CLOCKS & WATCHES

Compiled and Edited by
TONY CURTIS

First Published July 1976
Reprinted Dec. 1976
" April 1977
" Aug. 1977
Revised Edition June 1978

Exchange Rate $2 = £1

Original Edition ISBN 902921-44-4
Revised Edition ISBN 902921-70-3

Copyright © Lyle Publications 1977.
Published by Lyle Publications, Glenmayne, Galashiels, Scotland.
Distributed in the U.S.A. by Apollo, 391 South Road, Poughkeepsie, N.Y. 12601.

INTRODUCTION

Congratulations! You now have in your hands an extremely valuable book. It is one of a series specially devised to aid the busy professional dealer in his everyday trading. It will also prove to be of great value to all collectors and those with goods to sell, for it is crammed with illustrations, brief descriptions and valuations of hundreds of antiques.

Every effort has been made to ensure that each specialised volume contains the widest possible variety of goods in its particular category though the greatest emphasis is placed on the middle bracket of trade goods rather than on those once-in-a-lifetime museum pieces whose values are of academic rather than practical interest to the vast majority of dealers and collectors.

This policy has been followed as a direct consequence of requests from dealers who sensibly realise that, no matter how comprehensive their knowledge, there is always a need for reliable, up-to-date reference works for identification and valuation purposes.

When using your Antiques and their Values to assess the worth of goods, please bear in mind that it would be impossible to place upon any item a precise value which would hold good under all circumstances. No antique has an exactly calculable value; its price is always the result of a compromise reached between buyer and seller, and questions of condition, local demand and the business acumen of the parties involved in a sale are all factors which affect the assessment of an object's 'worth' in terms of hard cash.

In the final analysis, however, such factors cancel out when large numbers of sales are taken into account by an experienced valuer, and it is possible to arrive at a surprisingly accurate assessment of current values of antiques; an assessment which may be taken confidently to be a fair indication of the worth of an object and which provides a reliable basis for negotiation.

Throughout this book, objects are grouped under category headings and, to expedite reference, they progress in price order within their own categories. Where the description states 'one of a pair' the value given is that for the pair sold as such.

Printed by Apollo Press, Dominion Way, Worthing, Sussex, England.
Bound by Newdigate Press, Vincent Lane, Dorking, Surrey, England.

CONTENTS

BRACKET CLOCKS

Victorian oak cased striking bracket clock. $70 £35

Victorian striking bracket clock in a carved walnut case with a silvered dial. $70 £35

Late 19th century oak cased striking clock with a silvered dial. $70 £35

Victorian oak cased bracket clock with a brass and silvered dial and quarter chimes. $80 £40

Late 19th century carved mahogany cased bracket clock with a white enamel face by Elkington. $90 £45

Edwardian mahogany cased bracket clock with a silvered dial and Westminster chimes. $100 £50

Edwardian bracket clock in mahogany case with eight day French movement. $120 £60

Victorian mahogany cased bracket clock with musical chiming movement 52cm. $200 £1

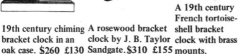

19th century chiming bracket clock in an oak case. $260 £130

A rosewood bracket clock by J. B. Taylor Sandgate. $310 £155

A 19th century French tortoise-shell bracket clock with brass mounts. $340 £170

A striking bracket clock in an ebonised case, by R. Bryson & Sons, Edinburgh, circa 1850. $340 £170

A Regency rose-wood bracket clock, with brass ring handles and ball feet, by J. Bates, Huddersfield, 15½ins. $360 £180

A fine bracket clock by J. Moore & Sons, Clerkenwell. $360 £180

19th century French ebonised bracket clock by A. Furet, Paris. 51cm. $360 £180

A carved oak bracket clock with musical striking movement, by Benson, London, 2ft. high $380 £190

Regency period mahogany cased bracket clock with an 8 day movement. $420 £210

18th century ebonised bracket clock with silverised and chased brass arched dial and second indicator. $430 £215

Early 19th century bracket clock in an ebonised case with brass string inlay. $440 £220

An Edwardian bracket clock with chime action. $460 £230

19th century Gothic style rosewood bracket clock. $590 £295

Mahogany 2 train clock by Jefferson of Bruton Street, London. $600 £300

Bracket clock by I.C. Fennens of London, circa 1850. $650 £325

A Regency bracket clock by Gravell & Son, London, in rosewood case on ball feet. $660 £330

9

BRACKET CLOCKS

19th century eight day English ebonised striking bracket clock with a brass face. $660 £330

Mahogany bracket clock by Gilson of Royal Exchange, with pull repeat, circa 1810. $670 £335

Mahogany bracket clock with inlaid cross decoration and a pineapple finial, by James McCabe. $680 £340

Mahogany cased two-train bracket clock by Shepheard of Plymouth, circa 1815. $710 £355

Regency mahogany bracket clock by James Murray with repeating movement, 1ft. 10ins. high. $720 £360

Mahogany cased bracket clock by A. Louis Breguet of Paris, circa 1815. $720 £360

A striking bracket clock in ebonised wood case by John Williamson, circa 1700. $720 £360

A yew wood bracket clock by Isaac Nickols of Wells, Somerset, 20 ins. $720

Striking Regency mahogany bracket clock by Runge. $740 £370

19th century bracket clock in ebonised case. $780 £390

Quarter chiming fusee movement bracket clock. $780 £390

Two train brack clock by J. Mee of London, circa 1810. $780 £3

10

Bracket clock by
P. Wood of London
in an ebonised case
with hour and pull
repeater quarter
strike, 22½ ins.
circa 1760. $800 £400

Regency bracket
clock by Elliot,
on scroll feet.
$840 £420

An ebonised
bracket clock,
with eight bell
chime, London
maker, unsigned.
$840 £420

18th century
bracket clock
in lacquered
case by J.
Wainwright,
Wellingborough,
with a brass
face. $840 £420

Regency bracket
clock by Grant
with brass inlaid
mahogany case.
$840 £420

Two train hour
repeating bracket
clock by Haddack
of Bath in maho-
gany case.
$850 £425

Mahogany bracket
clock with silvered
dial and lever
escapement, circa
1830. $880 £440

Good quality
bracket clock
with engraved
backplate and
pendulum,
circa 1815. $900
£450

Regency mahogany
bracket clock with
brass inlay, circa
1820. $900 £450

English striking
bracket clock
with silvered
dial. $900 £450

Regency bracket
clock with hour
strike and pull
repeat.
$920 £460

Georgian bracket
clock by J. Bennett
of London.
$920 £460

11

BRACKET CLOCKS

19th century rose-wood bracket clock with silent and chime on 8 bells, 32 ins high. $940 £470

George III mahogany balloon bracket clock by James Radford, with white painted dial, 1ft. 7ins. high. $960 £480

Bracket clock by Joseph Martineau Senr., of London. $980 £490

Mahogany and brass inlaid bracket clock by Viner of New Bond St. $1,010 £5

George III bracket clock by John Skinner, Exeter $1,010 £505

Three train bracket clock on 8 bells. $1,010 £505

George III bracket clock by J. Skinner Oxon. $1,010 £505

Mahogany bracket clock by J. Hardy & Co., Aberdeen, circa 1850, 28 in. $1,010 £

18th century ebon-ised bracket clock, by J. Fladgate, London, 18 ins. high $1,010 £505

18th century two train bracket clock with engra-ved back plate and hour repeat. $1,020 £510

Victorian ebon-ised bracket clock with a three train musical movement, 30 ins. $1,020 £510

Early 18th cen-tury bracket clock in an ebony veneered case, by T. Cliff of Hull. $1,020 £51

18th century mahogany table clock, by F. Miller of London, circa 1780. $1,020 £510

18th century bracket clock by Wright of London. $1,030 £515

18th century bracket clock by Peter Nichols of Newport. $1,030 £515

Ebonised bracket clock with 8 day movement by Jennens with Cambridge chimes. $1,040 £520

Early 19th century three train ebonised bracket clock. $1,080 £540

A late 18th century mahogany cased bracket clock by T. Simson. $1,080 £540

Verge bracket clock by J. Wilson, signed and numbered on dial and backplate. $1,120 £560

Mahogany bracket clock by A. Perinot of Paddington, circa 1760. $1,140 £570

Verge bracket clock by J. Wilson. $1,140 £570

Mid 18th century ebonised clock with engraved backplate. $1,140 £570

Mahogany bracket clock by J. Hardy & Co., Aberdeen, circa 1850, 28 ins. $1,150 £575

Mid 19th century ebony bracket clock, J. Vulliamy, London, numbered 571. $1,190 £595

BRACKET CLOCKS

Three train bracket clock chiming on quarters on either four or eight bells. **$1,200 £600**

Late 18th century mahogany cased bracket clock by W. Shilling of Milton. **$1,200 £600**

Georgian bracket clock by James McCabe of London, in a red walnut case. **$1,200 £600**

18th century mahogany bracket clock by Bryant & Son, London 1781, 19½ ins. **$1,200 £600**

18th century mahogany bracket clock with domed top by G. F. Coldway, Strand, London. **$1,200 £600**

19th century bracket clock chiming on 8 bells and Westminster chimes. **$1,250 £625**

George III bracket clock by Edmund Pistor of London. **$1,260 £630**

19th century Viennese bracket clock in a gilt case. **$1,280 £640**

Red walnut bracket clock with musical striking movement, inscribed H. J. Taylor. **$1,300 £650**

Mahogany cased bracket clock by E. Tutet, Jnr. of London. **$1,300 £650**

George III bracket clock in a mahogany case by Allen and Clements. **$1,320 £660**

18th century mahogany bracket clock with brass inset spandrels by J. Cowan, Edin. **$1,390 £6**

14

Verge bracket clock, in ebonised case, with silvered brass dial, by R.Ward, London. **$1,430 £715**

Rosewood striking bracket clock by Brockbank and Atkins.**$1,450 £725**

Late 18th century mahogany cased bracket clock by E. Edlyne of London. **$1,490 £745**

Bell quarter repeat bracket clock in a fruitwood case, 12 ins. **$1,500 £750**

Verge escapement bracket clock by Alderslade of Islington, circa 1790.**$1,500 £750**

Bracket clock by W. Tomlinson,in a figured walnut case.**$1,500 £750**

Mahogany bracket clock by T. York of London, circa 1780, 16 ins. **$1,520 £760**

18th century bracket clock. **$1,560 £780**

Verge bracket timepiece by J. Hewlett of Bristol. **$1,620 £810**

18th century bracket clock in pearwood by J. McCabe, Royal Exchange, London. **$1,680 £840**

Mahogany cased bracket clock by Septucius Miles, Ludgate St., London. **$1,760 £880**

Mahogany verge bracket clock with strike silent regulation, by Winch of Maidenhead. **$1,790 £895**

15

BRACKET CLOCKS

Bracket clock by J. Cowan of Edinburgh in an ebonised case. $1,800 £900

A ¼ pull repeat bracket clock by R. Rouch of Bristol in an ebonised case, circa 1760. $1,800 £900

George I three train quarter chime bracket clock in mahogany case. $1,800 £900

Fine early 18th century bracket clock by Sam Humphreys of London. $1,800 £900

Three-train ebonised bracket clock, quarter chiming on four gongs with pull quarter repeat. $1,860 £930

Bracket clock by T. Mudge of London in a walnut case, 13½ ins high. $1,860 £930

Mahogany bracket clock with strike/silent regulation by P. Gullock, Rochford, circa 1785 $1,860 £930

Ebonised two-train bracket clock with anchor escapement. $1,910 £955

18th century mahogany bracket clock by J. Cole of Stowey, Somerset. $1,910 £955

George III mahogany bracket clock by John Prichard 1ft. 10½ins. high. $2,160 £1,080

A mahogany bracket clock by T. Mudge and W. Dutton, London. $2,160 £1,080

Ebonised fruitwood bracket clock by Coleman, London, circa 1790. $2,160 £1,080

16

18th century mahogany bracket clock with silvered dial by T. West, Reading, 1775, 20 ins. high. $2,180 £1,090

Mahogany verge timepiece alarm, signed Grant, Fleet Street, London. $2,280 £1,140

Superb bracket clock in an ebonised case by T. Smith of Norwich. $2,350 £1,175

Ebonised two-train clock with strike silent regulation by W. Barry of London, circa 1790. $2,390 £1,195

A good musical bracket clock by J. Evans, 15½ ins. high. $2,420 £1,210

An 18th century bracket clock by Williamson of London, 12 ins. $2,420 £1,210

18th century three train bracket clock by C. Dunlop of London, 22 ins. high. $2,420 £1,210

Mahogany cased eight day bracket clock, 18 ins. $2,750 £1,375

Bracket clock by G. Lindsay of London, circa 1770. $2,970 £1,485

Good 18th century ebonised bracket clock by W. Pride of Sarum, circa 1750. $3,190 £1,595

Fine bracket clock by J. Gerrard. $3,300 £1,650

Rare bracket clock by G. Mondi in a walnut veneered case, circa 1700. $3,300 £1,650

BRACKET CLOCKS

An early 18th century bracket clock by William Marshall of Dublin. $3,630 £1,815

Rare Anglo-Dutch ebonised table clock by Robert Hodgkin of London, circa 1700. $3,740 £1,870

Fine quality George III bracket clock by Stephen Rimbault of London. $3,850 £1,925

A three train chiming bracket clock by William Sutton of London. $3,850 £1,925

Late 17th century bracket clock with original verge escapement by Gabriel Smith Bathomley, circa 1695, 14ins. high. $4,070 £2,035

A mid 18th century bracket clock with verge escapement and engraved backplate, 18ins. high. $4,070 £2,035

Rare Queen Anne bracket clock by Peter King of London, with verge escapement and engraved backplate, circa 1710. $4,400 £2,200

An ebonised bracket clock by Claude Du Chesne, London, 42cm. high. $4,950 £2,475

Ebonised bracket clock with verge escapement by John Hoddle of Reading, circa 1690 $5,390 £2,695

A fine ebonised bracket clock by John Elsworth of London circa 1690 $5,500 £2,750

Figured walnut bracket clock by John Ellicott, circa 1740. $5,720 £2,860

Early 19th century musical bracket clock, dead beat escapement, by Gravel and Tolkein. $6,270 £3,135

An early pull quarter repeat timepiece, with finely engraved backplate, by Jacobus Goubert, circa 1685. $6,490 £3,245

Regency musical bracket clock with quarter striking eight tunes on twelve bells, by Frodsham, London, circa 1825, 36in. $6,600 £3,300

Late 17th century ebonised bracket clock by Jacobus Goubert, London, 12ins. high. $6,600 £3,300

A 17th century ebonised bracket clock by Jonathan Lowndes of Pall Mall, circa 1690, 12½ins. high. $7,260 £3,630

Very small 17th century basket top timepiece by D. Threlkeld of Newcastle, circa 1685. $7,370 £3,685

Bracket clock by Ellicott, London, circa 1770, striking on thirteen bells, 65cm. high. $7,480 £3,740

18th century bracket clock by Paul Rimbault of London. $7,920 £3,960

A very rare twelve tune musical and automata ebonised bracket clock, circa 1760, 25ins. high. $8,250 £4,125

Ebonised table clock the movement with verge escapement, $8,470 £4,235

A red tortoiseshell bracket clock, by Marshall, Dublin, 1/00, 15½ins.high $9,800 £4,900

Early 18th century ebonised bracket clock by Daniel Quare of London, circa 1720. $12,100 £6,050

An eight day alarm timepiece by George Graham, 12ins. high. $15,000 £7,500

19

BRACKET CLOCKS

Bracket clock by Daniel Quare with a repeating alarm, $17,600 £8,800

A small ebony veneered table clock with original verge escapement, signed Joseph Knibb, Londini fecit, 11¾ ins. high, circa 1685. $20,800 £10,400

A fine walnut bracket clock by Joseph Knibb, with cherub spandrels and engraved back-plate. $24,200 £12,100

Small table clock by Thomas Tompion. $26,400 £13,200

Late 17th century bracket clock by Joseph Knibb, London, case of ebonised wood, 33.5cm. high. $27,500 £13,750

A walnut, quarter-repeating bracket timepiece by Thomas Tompion, 12½ins. high. $33,000 £16,500

An ebony cased quarter-repeating bracket clock by Thomas Tompion, 14¾ins. high, circa 1700 $34,100 £17,050

A very fine bracket clock by Daniel Quare. $35,200 £17,60

Early 18th century gilt-metal clock with musical repeat movement by William Webster, London, 47cm. high. $42,000 £21,000

A bracket clock by Thomas Tompion London, circa 1698, 40 cm. high $44,000 £22,000

A fine bracket clock by Thomas Tompion circa 1680-85, 32 cm high $56,000 £28,000

An ebony veneer-ed bracket clock by G. Graham with a quarter repeating mech-anism, 10 in. high. $80,000 £40,000

20

A French carriage clock in brass and glazed case, 4¼ins. high. **$120 £60**

A carriage clock with white enamelled dial by Parkins & Co., London, 3½ins. high. **$150 £75**

A French carriage clock in brass case, 4½ins. high. **$160 £80**

A miniature carriage clock in brass and glazed case, 2¾ins. high. **$200 £100**

A carriage clock with white enamel dial, in brass case, 3ins. high. **$220 £110**

Modern English carriage clock by W.J. Huber, 16.5cm. high. **$220 £110**

Small Victorian eight day carriage clock. **$240 £120**

Victorian brass carriage clock with an eight day movement. **$240 £120**

Late 19th century timepiece with original cylinder escapement. **$250 £125**

A French carriage clock with white enamel dial, by J. Bennet, 5ins. high. **$250 £125**

Small Victorian brass carriage clock with Roman numerals. **$260 £130**

Small Victorian brass carriage clock with an eight day move-ment. **$260 £130**

21

CARRIAGE CLOCKS

French cylinder movement carriage clock circa 1910, 14cm. $280 £140

A French carriage striking clock in brass and glazed case, 5 ins. $300 £150

Victorian brass carriage clock timepeice, circa 1850. $300 £150

19th century carriage time-piece, with original lever escapement. $300 £150

Late 19th century French brass carriage clock with alarm. $300 £150

Gilt metal and bevelled glass cased carriage timepiece, 4½ ins. high. $300 £150

French carriage clock with alarm, circa 1920, 10cm high. $320 £160

Miniature carriage timepiece contained in a gilt metal case, 3ins. high. $320 £160

Cased timepiece with 'bettle and poker' hands, 5ins. $340 £170

Victorian brass carriage clock with a lever movement and repeater. $350 £175

Victorian carriage clock with enamel and brass dial and fluted pillars, 13cm. high. $350 £175

Timepiece in satin gilt case, the back plate signed with a 'stalking lion', 4½ ins. $350 £175

22

A small 19th century cased carriage clock. $350 £175

A French carriage striking clock, in a brass case, 5ins. high. $350 £175

Late 19th century timepiece/alarm, with original lever escapement. $360 £180

Small 19th century French brass carriage clock in a serpentine shaped case. $370 £185

19th century French carriage clock in an oval shaped brass case, 6ins. high. $370 £185

An unusual 19th century twin carriage clock and barometer by Spaulding & Co., Paris. $370 £185

An early miniature timepiece/alarm, in satin gilt case, alarm sounds on bell. $380 £190

An early alarm carriage clock, with enamel face and cylinder escapement. $380 £190

A plain striking clock with replacement lever escapement, 4½ ins. high. $380 £190

Good quality timepiece in gorge case, probably by Drocourt, No. 30928. $380 £190

Victorian brass carriage clock with a green enamel dial, ½ hour strike and alarm. $380 £190

23

CARRIAGE CLOCKS

An oval timepiece below which is an aneroid barometer, with thermometers at either side, 6¾in. **$400 £200**

An extremely small, square cased miniature timepiece, numbered A. 572. **$400 £200**

An unusual combination timepiece with aneroid barometer by Richard Et Cie, Paris, 5 ins. **$420 £210**

Gilt metal cased repeating alarm carriage clock 5¾ ins. **$430 £2**

Miniature gilt cased alarm carriage timepiece, 3 ins. high. **$430 £215**

Miniature French timepiece in silver, hallmarked 1899, 11.5cm high. **$440 £220**

A French Champleve enamel brass carriage clock, with bevel glazed door, standing on bun feet, circa 1900. **$440 £220**

19th century brass carriage clock with chased case and decorated dial. **$460 £230**

Timepiece in gilt and cloisonne enamelled case. 5ins high. **$480 £240**

Miniature timepiece, with cylinder movement, 2¾ins. **$490 £245**

Striking clock on gong with excellent gilt case work, No. 1634. **$490 £245**

24

A miniature brass carriage clock, with a lever movement, the base marked Claude No. 380. $500 £250

19th century rosewood cased calendar carriage clock by Reynolds of London. $500 £250

English gilt brass carriage clock with repeat and alarm, circa 1880. $500 £250

A brass carriage clock, striking the quarter hour with a repeating movement. $500 £250

Late 19th century French enamel brass carriage clock with pastoral scenes, on bracket feet. $500 £250

Late 19th century Champleve enamel carriage clock with white enamel dial. $520 £260

Miniature carriage clock by Margaine, timepiece only. $530 £265

A small repeater carriage clock of high quality, 4½ins. $550 £275

Timepiece in unusual gilt case in 'Palladian' style. $550 £275

Gilt metal cased repeating carriage clock. 6ins. $550 £275

A miniature timepiece of pagoda shape, with enamelled dial, 3¾ins. $580 £290

A miniature timepiece of elegant proportion, 3ins. high. $580 £290

CARRIAGE CLOCKS

Mid 19th century English carriage clock with repeater and alarm, numbered 396 and with initials JS. $580 £290

Brass cased repeater carriage clock with lever movement. $580 £290

Gilt metal cased lever movement carriage clock. $580 £290

19th century French brass carriage clock with a cloisonne enamel centre panel. $600 £300

A fine repeater carriage clock by Richard et Cie, Paris, No. 277, in a brass case. $610 £305

Victorian brass carriage clock with full repeating sonnerie movement on two gongs. $610 £305

A most unusual striking clock on bell, with early escapement featuring both alarm and rare sweep seconds hand. $650 £325

Serpentine front brass cased carriage clock with lever movement. $650 £325

19th century repeater carriage clock of good quality in a brass case. $650 £325

Cylindrical brass cased carriage with lever movement. $670 £335

Miniature ¼ repeat carriage clock with a blue enamel face, complete with travelling case. $680 £340

19th century gilt soft metal carriage clock with repeat and alarm. $720 £360

An oval brass framed carriage clock with strike and repeating movement, circa 1870. $740 £370

A striking clock by H. Et Cie, Paris, helical balance spring with bridge platform, circa 1820. $740 £370

Edwardian striking carriage clock with enamel dial and sides in a brass case. $790 £395

A repeater carriage clock in a fluted matt gilt case, with replacement platform, 6 ins. $800 £400

French strike repeat carriage clock with alarm, circa 1880, 16.5cm. $800 £400

An elegant repeater carriage clock in fine quality gilded case, unsigned. $800 £400

An English cased carriage clock with an engraved dial mask and very rare bottom winding handles, circa 1850. $840 £420

A repeater carriage clock, the gilt dial plate with white enamelled chapter ring, 5½ins. $890 £445

19th century brass cased repeater carriage clock. $890 £445

An oval strike and repeat carriage clock. $890 £445

An early repeater carriage clock by Japy Freres Et Cie, signed, with cylinder escapement. $900 £450

A mid 19th century half hour striking repeating carriage clock with alarm, inscribed Dent a Paris. $900 £450

CARRIAGE CLOCKS

A French brass carriage clock with a movement by Pons, engraved with scrolling foliage, 5½ins. high. $910 £455

An interesting calendar timepiece, with silvered engraved dial plate and chapter ring at top by Baveaux, 5½ins. high. $920 £460

Brass carriage clock, French, eight day repeating movement with alarm, No. 2034. $940 £470

An attractively cased repeater carriage clock with white enamelled face, No. 338. $950 £475

Repeating carriage alarm clock with decorative porcelain panels, 6½in. high. $960 £480

Early striker on bell in fine cast case by Bolviller, Paris, with cylinder escapement and beautifully engraved platform, 5¾ins. high $960 £480

A calendar carriage timepiece with an enamel dial, 6in. high. $1,010 £505

An unusual French carriage clock in an ormolu case, 10ins. high. $1,030 £515

Small eight day French grandesonnerie carriage clock. $1,030 £515

A fine quarter striking and repeat carriage clock by Margaine, with subsiduary alarm. $1,070 £535

French strike repeat carriage clock, circa 1880, 18cm. high, with corinthian pilasters $1,080 £540

A French travelling clock, 8ins. high, the case with pierced friezes and columns $1,100 £5

An early repeater alarm carriage clock, by George Jamieson, Paris, with cylinder escapement, striking on bell, 5¼ins. high, circa 1830. $1,120 £560

An oval cased hour and half hour strike and repeat carriage clock, 6ins. high. $1,160 £580

A very fine repeater carriage clock of simple design, in matt gilded case, with alarm numbered 6224 $1,160 £580

A late 18th century brass travelling clock by Mayr Karlsbaad, 18cm. high. $1,200 £600

repeater carriage clock in a matt gilded case, with silver dial, by Margaine (signed), ¾ins. high $1,220 £610

A repeater carriage clock in architectural case with fretted gilt overlay, numbered 202. $1,250 £625

Grande sonnerie carriage clock by Dixon of Norwich. $1,250 £625

Gilt framed chiming carriage clock decorated with mosaic birds and foliage. $1,250 £625

19th century baroque French carriage clock by Japy Freres. $1,250 £625

An unusual example of a Petit-sonnerie by A. Magraine, without a strike/silent control, 5ins. high. $1,270 £635

Engraved striking and repeating alarm carriage clock, circa 1850, 7¾ins. high. $1,360 £680

A fine quality 19th century French carriage clock by Leroy et Fils of Paris. $1,380 £690

29

CARRIAGE CLOCKS

A striking clock signed by Henri Mare, Paris, having helical balance spring with bridge platform, circa 1835. $1,400 £700

Japanese brass clock contained in a hardwood cabinet with glazed panels, 12.5cm. high.
$1,540 £770

French striking clock by Leroy et Fils, circa 1845, 13cm. high.
$1,620 £81

An important repeater carriage clock, by Paul Garnie with Chaff-Cutter escapement striking on bell, 5ins. high. $1,620 £810

French timepiece with fusee movement, circa 1880, 14cm. high.
$1,620 £810

A fine oval Petit-Sonnerie by Richard et Cie (signed), with white enamelled dial, 5½ins. high. $1,620 £810

Early 19th century repeater carriage clock with alarm.
$1,680 £84

Fine English fusee carriage clock by A. De Boos, London, with gilt engine-turned case, circa 1830.
$1,700 £850

A small grande-sonnerie carriage clock with masked dial and alarm, 4½ins. high.
$1,780 £890

French carriage clock with wheel striking and lever escapement, circa 1840, 12.5cm. high.
$1,800 £900

Corinthian columned case grande-sonnerie carriage clock, 6½ins. high.
$1,800 £900

Grande-Sonnerie by Richard et Cie (signed), striking on gong, gilt gorge case, with white enamelled dial.
$1,860 £930

A fine grande sonnerie carriage clock with fretted and engraved mask to blue enamel dial.
$1,860 £930

Repeating alarm French carriage clock in an elaborate ormolu case, 8in. high.
$1,870 £935

A fine repeater carriage clock decorated with porcelain panels, signed David Keys, Paris. **$1,870 £935**

A small gilt metal carriage clock signed Leroy et Fils, with gilt filigree decoration, 4ins. high. **$1,970 £985**

French strike, repeat, carriage clock with alarm, circa 1850, in a rococo case, 11.5cm. high. **$2,040 £1,020**

A French brass oval carriage clock by Drocourt, 15cm. high. **$2,160 £1,080**

Brass framed carriage clock decorated with handpainted porcelain panels, by T. Detardin, circa 1875. **$2,160 £1,080**

th century engraved rriage clock with a er movement, push eat, alarm and grande nnerie, 6ins. high. **$2,160 £1,080**

French carriage clock with grande sonnerie and alarm, circa 1875, 15cm. high. **$2,160 £1,080**

Superb grande sonnerie carriage clock by Drocourt, signed on dial and underneath. **$2,200 £1,100**

An unusual repeater carriage clock with moon phase aperture by Henri Marc. **$2,280 £1,140**

31

CARRIAGE CLOCKS

Fine Georgian carriage clock by James McCabe of London.
$2,400 £1,200

Carriage clock by E. White, London, gilt engine-turned case, with subsidiary seconds dial, 5ins. high, circa 1820.
$2,400 £1,200

A very fine grande sonnerie, unsigned, No. 3827, with an alarm and striking on gong, 6¼ins. high.$2,520 £1,260

An exceptional miniature repeater by Drocourt, numbered 32509 striking hours and half hours. 3ins. high. $2,520 £1,

French strike repeat carriage clock with alarm. circa 1890, 24cm. high, in a cloisonne enamel case.$2,650 £1,325

Strike and repeat carriage clock in fine quality brass case, with alarm and music box mechanism. $2,750 £1,375

A repeater/alarm carriage clock with painted Sevres panels overlaid with gilt fretting, 5¾ins. high.
$2,860 £1,430

A repeater/alarm carriage clock in a hexagonal case with barley-twist columns, unsigned 6ins. high. $2,97 £1,

Early 19th century French grande sonnerie carriage clock by Leroy et Fils of Paris.
$3,080 £1,540

A gilt metal carriage timepiece with an enamel dial, 6½ ins. high, by Dent.
$3,300 £1,650

Miniature French timepiece by Leroy et Fils, circa 1880, with pietra dura panels of birds and flowers.
$3,300 £1,650

A French carriage clock, the movement contained in a gorge case inset with porcelain.
$3,960 £1,980

French carriage clock with petit sonnerie and alarm by Leroy et Fils, circa 1870, 15cm. high.
$4,290 £2,145

A superb repeater and strike twin fusee carriage clock by James McCabe, 6ins. high, circa 1815. $5,280 £2,640

Singing bird carriage clock with alarm by Japy Freres, 29.2cm. high. $5,500 £2,750

19th century minute repeating French carriage clock by Hunt & Roskell. $5,500 £2,750

French grande sonnerie with alarm by Drocourt, circa 1880, with simulated bamboo pilasters and enamel case, 17.1cm. high. $5,500 £2,750

English striking carriage clock signed Barwise, London, 1845, with an engraved case. $9,900 £4,950

A very fine Breguet brass-cased carriage clock with repeater and alarm movement, 5½ins. high. $11,000 £5,500

19th century silver grand sonnerie Tourbillon clock by Vicole Niel-son $12,010 £6,005

nglish strike repeat riage clock by nt, London, in a thic case, 21cm. h $13,200 £6,600

English carriage clock by Jump, London, dated 1885 with striking movement and hour repeat. $13,200 £6,600

An exceptionally fine carriage clock by Frederick Dent. $28,000 £14,000

A silver-cased grande sonnerie carriage clock. $33,500 £16,750

33

CLOCK SETS

19th century rouge marble clock with a pair of matching side pieces, 10 ins high. $120 £60

A black slate clock set, inlaid with marble and with white enamel circular dial. $150 £75

An Art Deco soft metal clock set, complete with side urns. $240 £120

Victorian garniture de cheminee comprising a marble cased clock with bronze mounts, surmounted by a seated scholar in classical robes. With matching urns. $300 £

A French bronze and porcelain clock set, the dial and side panels painted with figures by H. Desprey, the clock 15 ins, the two vases 10½ ins. $330 £165

A brass mantel clock set, the clock with enamel dial and the vases with covers, 10 ins. $350 £175

A French brass garniture de cheminee of clock with two figures of Roman soldiers and a pair of double handled vases, the clock 13 ins, vases 8½ ins. $440 £220

French Empire ormolu and blue porcelain garniture de cheminee. $440 £220

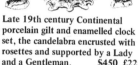

Late 19th century Continental porcelain gilt and enamelled clock set, the candelabra encrusted with rosettes and supported by a Lady and a Gentleman. $450 £225

Brass garniture de cheminee with coloured enamel mounts. French clock 11½ins., and pair of urn-shaped vases 8½ins. $480 £240

A 19th century French clock set in ormolu with decorative porcelain plaques. $500 £250

A fine Louis XV style ormolu clock set, by J.P. Japy, with striking movement, circa 1878. $600 £300

35

19th century French clock set, in marble and ormolu, with hour and half-hour strike, circa 1870. $600 £300

19th century three piece gilded clock set decorated with porcelain panels. $620 £310

19th century French ormolu clock set by Robin a Paris, 12in. $620 £310

Early 19th century Empire style white marble and ormolu clock set. $620 £310

Louis XVI style gilt metal clock set, inset with china plaques, the clock 22ins. high, the vases 18ins. high. $620 £310

19th century French marble and ormolu mounted striking clock. $710 £355

19th century French rouge marble and ormolu mounted striking clock with matching side pieces, 11 ins. $780 £390

Three piece white marble and ormolu clock set, circa 1860. $800 £400

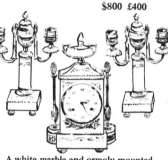

19th century three piece clock set in onyx with cloisonne decoration. $820 £410

A white marble and ormolu mounted French clock with an 8 day movement and a pair of candelabra cassolet side-pieces, circa 1860. $820 £410

A French Empire style gilt metal clock set, the clock 17¼ ins, the two vases 12½ ins. $820 £410

19th century vase shaped clock set in bleu de roi mounted with ormolu. $840 £420

CLOCK SETS

Three-piece marble and ormolu clock set. $910 £455

A fine clock set, in basalt, bronze and gilt. $960 £480

A good 18th century Sevres garniture de cheminee decorated with male and female figures in ormolu. $960 £480

Regency bronze and ormolu clock set, by French of the Royal Exchange London. $960 £480

19th century bronzed and ormolu, three piece white marble ball clock set, 14ins. high. $960 £480

19th century dark blue porcelain and ormolu mounted clock set, with hand painted panels in the style of Sevres. $960 £48

Mid 19th century clock set comprising a pair of cast brass candelabra and a cast brass clock in the shape of a church. $1,020 £510

A three piece green onyx marble and porcelain clock set with ormolu mounts, circa 1860. $1,020 £510

A good quality mid 19th century ormolu bronze and white marble ball clock set, 14 ins high. $1,020 £510

19th century French ormolu clock with a pair of matching ormolu candelabra. $1,080 £540

Small white marble and ormolu mounted French striking clock by Vincent, circa 1860, with pair of matching candelabra sidepieces. $1,140 £570

Superb quality early 19th century ormolu and chinoiserie striking clock complete with side ornaments. $1,160 £580

CLOCK SETS

A white onyx, marble and ormolu
French striking clock with matching
side pieces.　　　　$1,190 £595

An unusual Lyre shaped white
marble and ormolu mounted
French clock set. $1,200 £600

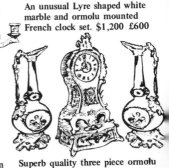

Early 19th century ormolu Dolphin
mounted clock set on a green marble
base.　　　　$1,220 £610

Superb quality three piece ormolu
mounted, hand painted, blue Sevres
porcelain clock set by Vincente,
13½ins. high.　　　　$1,260 £630

An ormolu and cloisonne enamel
French striking clock with porcelain
panels with a pair of complementary
ormolu and porcelain side pieces,
15ins. high, circa 1860. $1,260 £630

Finely chased rococo style ormolu
French striking clock by Mougin,
circa 1860, with matching side-
pieces, 14in high x 11in wide x
8in deep.　　　　$1,320 £660

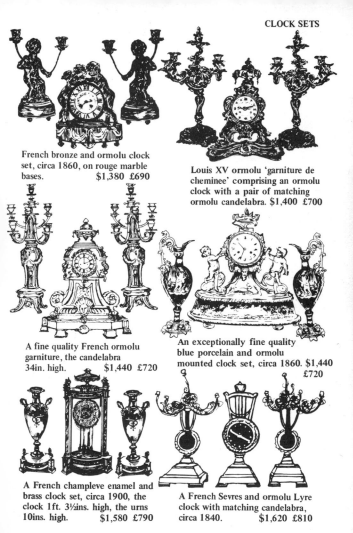

French bronze and ormolu clock set, circa 1860, on rouge marble bases. $1,380 £690

Louis XV ormolu 'garniture de cheminee' comprising an ormolu clock with a pair of matching ormolu candelabra. $1,400 £700

A fine quality French ormolu garniture, the candelabra 34in. high. $1,440 £720

An exceptionally fine quality blue porcelain and ormolu mounted clock set, circa 1860. $1,440 £720

A French champleve enamel and brass clock set, circa 1900, the clock 1ft. 3½ins. high, the urns 10ins. high. $1,580 £790

A French Sevres and ormolu Lyre clock with matching candelabra, circa 1840. $1,620 £810

41

CLOCK SETS

19th century French gilt metal and white marble garniture de cheminee.
$1,680 £840

French ormolu and cloisonne clock set, circa 1860. $1,800 £900

Early 19th century ormolu garniture de cheminee, comprising a cherub mounted clock set, and a pair of candelabra. $2,020 £1,010

A superb quality ormolu and Sevres porcelain clock set with handpainted panels depicting flowers and putti, by Japy Freres. $2,400 £1,200

A 19th century French ormolu and champleve enamel garniture.
$2,500 £1,250

A 19th century clock garniture, the clock 17in. high. $3,740 £1,

An oak cased grandmother musical chiming clock. $120 £60

Enfield Westminster chime grandmother clock in an oak case. $150 £75

Late 19th century art deco clock in an oak case. $220 £110

Oak cased grandmother clock with Westminster chime. $220 £110

orge III painted e eight day grand- her clock in an case. $240 £120

19th century mahogany longcase clock, with circular enamel dial, by Wm. Young, Dundee. $260 £130

Early 19th century mahogany cased grandfather clock with a painted face and eight day movement. $270 £135

Oak cased eight day painted face grandfather clock, by Kemp of Oxford. $270 £135

GRANDFATHER CLOCKS

Late 18th century oak cased clock by Watkin Owen, with a brass dial. $270 £135

Early 19th century oak cased grandfather clock by Thomas Russel, with painted face. $270 £135

19th century mahogany longcase clock with eight day striking movement. $270 £135

Late 18th century longcase clock by Waldre of Arundel, with a white enamel face and oak case. $270 £13

Late Georgian country oak longcase clock of eight day duration. $270 £135

Early 19th century longcase clock with shaped pediment and eight day movement. $270 £135

Late 18th century oak cased eight day grandfather clock. $280 £140

19th century oak cased grandfather clock with a pair face and eight day movement. $300 £

44

George IV oak long-case clock, arched painted enamel dial, engraved Greig, Perth, 6ft.9ins. high. $320 £160

A mahogany long-case clock with brass dial and second movement by Mitchell & Sons, Glasgow. $320 £160

Victorian mahogany longcase clock, the enamel dial engraved Wm. Anders, St. Andrews. $320 £160

A 19th century oak longcase clock with scroll cresting and painted enamel arched dial. $340 £170

Late 18th century longcase clock with painted face and carved oak case by William Unwin. $340 £170

19th century oak longcase clock with second and calendar movements, by Jn. McCall, Dalkeith. $340 £170

Late 18th century brass faced eight day grandfather clock in an oak case. $350 £175

A mahogany grand-mother clock with chased brass and silverised dial. $360 £180

45

GRANDFATHER CLOCKS

An oak longcase clock signed Walker of Loughborough. **$400 £200**

Mahogany longcase clock of 8 day duration by George of Fishguard. **$400 £200**

George III mahogany longcase clock the dial signed W. Brownlie, Hamilton, 7ft. high. **$400 £200**

18th century inlaid and feathered mahogany longcase clock, with Corinthian pillar decoration and painted dial. **$400 £20**

A Victorian oak inlaid longcase clock, the painted enamel dial with figures of the Continents. **$400 £200**

19th century oak longcase clock with arched dial by G. Lowe, Dalkeith. **$400 £200**

An oak cased longcase clock inscribed Grice. **$410 £205**

Mahogany longcase clock inscribed Sic-Est Vita Hominis.**$420 £2**

Victorian mahogany longcase clock by G. White, Glasgow. $420 £210

18th century black lacquer, 30 hour clock by J. Marr of Retford. $420 £210

Mahogany longcase clock, with painted enamel dial, calendar and second movement, by J. Allan, Kilmarnock. $420 £210

18th century longcase clock by G. Bennett of Malmesbury. $440 £220

George III oak longcase clock by C. Cooper, circa 1780. $440 £220

A mahogany longcase clock with painted enamel dial, by G. Stonehouse, Newcastle. $450 £225

Regency period mahogany cased grandfather clock with an enamel dial. $450 £225

19th century oak longcase clock with Westminster chime. $460 £230

GRANDFATHER CLOCKS

Mahogany long-case clock by W. Theobold of Burneside. $480 £240

A 'Yorkshire' long-case clock by W. Massey of Nantwich. $480 £240

George III oak long-case clock by Dickerson of Egremont, circa 1790. $480 £240

Mahogany long-case clock with brass circular dial by J. Brydon, Dalkeith. $480 £240

18th century inlaid mahogany long-case clock. $530 £265

An oak longcase clock with eight day movement, signed Scorpion Southwell. $560 £280

18th century Scottish oak longcase clock by R. Knox, Steuarton. $560 £280

Mid 18th century oak cased Yorkshire grandfather clock. $560 £28

48

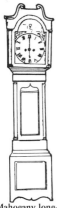

Mahogany long-case clock with arched dial by J. Templeton, Maybole. $580 £290

18th century inlaid oak eight day longcase clock with brass dial. $590 £295

Late 18th century carved oak eight day longcase clock with a brass dial. $590 £295

Mid 18th century mahogany longcase clock by John Owen of Llanwrst. $600 £300

18th century inlaid oak eight day long-case clock with a brass dial. $610 £305

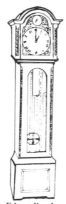

Edwardian longcase clock in a glazed oak case. $620 £310

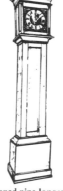

Stripped pine longcase clock, with single hand and brass dial by R. Felton, Bridnorth. $650 £325

19th century carved oak striking clock with 8 day movement. $660 £330

49

GRANDFATHER CLOCKS

18th century eight day longcase clock in a carved oak case. $660 £330

Longcase clock by J. Menzies, Perth, circa 1820, in a finely figured mahogany case. $660 £330

Late 18th century mahogany cased eight day grandfather clock with satinwood inlay. $660 £330

Good quality Scottish longcase clock, circa 1830. $660 £330

18th century mahogany cased grandfather clock with a brass dial. $660 £330

18th century oak longcase clock with engraved brass dial by Dickinson. $670 £335

Mahogany longcase clock with string inlay, by W. & C. Nicolas of Birmingham, circa 1840. $680 £340

Thirty hour longcase clock by J. Copper of Whitchurch, with fine spandrels, circa 1750 $680 £340

18th century long-case clock by D. Pallet, London, $700 £350

30 hour longcase clock in a lac-quered pine case by W. Barrow, London $720 £360

A mahogany long-case clock, the waist with Corin-thian columns, by J. Hamilton $720 £360

Oak longcase clock by M. Lyon, Lanark. $720 £360

Oak eight day longcase clock by John Smith of London. $720 £360

18th century brass faced grandfather clock with an eight day movement set in a fruitwood case. $720 £360

18th century car-ved oak grand-father clock by J. Hoddy of London. $780 £390

20th century long-case clock with Westminster and St Michael chimes. $780 £390

51

GRANDFATHER CLOCKS

An oak long-cased clock by Stevenson, Drayton, with brass face, 82 ins. $780 £390

Marble and bronze clock made for the Exposition Universalle, Paris 1878, 10ft. high. $840 £420

Late 17th century oak longcase clock by H. Montlow with a brass face and an eight day movement. $840 £420

Late 18th century longcase clock with eight day striking movement by G. Mawman, Beverley. $860 £43

A longcase clock by O. Brandreth of Middlewich, in an oak case crossbanded in mahogany, circa 1770. $900 £450

Late 18th century mahogany cased grandfather clock on ogee feet.
$900 £450

18th century longcase clock by R. Sadler, London. $910 £455

An eight day longcase clock by T. Baker, Portsmouth $910 £455

52

18th century mahogany longcase clock, with brass and silvered dial and brass weights. $920 £460

A mahogany longcase clock with semi-regulator movement by Brock, Lewisham, circa 1830. $950 £475

18th century mahogany longcase clock with a silvered arched dial by J. Stone of Madehurst. $960 £480

Mahogany longcased clock by J. Nottle of Okehampton. $1,010 £505

19th century mahogany 8 day striking clock by J. Begg, Glasgow. $1,020 £510

Walnut grandmother clock with weight driven short drop 8 day movement. $1,020 £510

Mahogany cased grandfather clock by R. Moxham of Coleford. $1,020 £510

Mid 18th century Comtoise or Morbier longcase clock with three train movement. $1,020 £510

GRANDFATHER CLOCKS

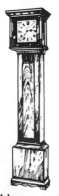

Mahogany grand-mother clock with early 19th century weight-driven move-ment and later case. $1,020 £510

Inlaid mahogany longcase clock with strike/silent regulation. $1,020 £510

Longcase clock by Cowsin of Lincoln, with broken arch pediment. $1,060 £530

Mahogany long-case clock with a brass eagle finial with out-stretched wings by Stripling, Litchfield. $1,060 £530

Longcase clock by F. Greg, with a lacquered case and brass face. $1,080 £540

Black lacquer long-case clock by T. Moore, Ipswich,, 1720-1789. $1,140 £570

A quarter chim-ing grandmother clock in walnut case. $1,140 £570

Walnut and mahogany miniature longcase clock by P. Brown of Manchester, 3ft 6ins high, circa 1850. $1,140 £570

54

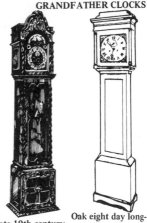

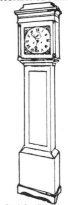

Regency clock with brass face by W. Phillip of Edinburgh, circa 1815 $1,140 £570

18th century black lacquered longcase clock by Richard Howard of Brentford. $1,250 £625

Late 19th century chiming longcase clock of Jacobean design. $1,250 £625

Oak eight day longcase clock by Snelling of Alton. $1,260 £630

18th century eight day clock by J. Wyld of Nottingham. $1,310 £655

Mahogany longcase clock by G. Negus of Huntingdon, circa 1795. $1,320 £660

19th century mahogany longcase clock by Wm. Greenwood, Leeds. $1,340 £670

Mahogany longcase clock, 8 day, circa 1770 $1,340 £670

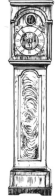

Regulator longcase clock by George Harvey, Edinburgh, circa 1825, in mahogany case. 84ins. high. $1,380 £690

Chippendale style mahogany clock by Taylor of Whitehaven (Cumberland), circa 1775, 7ft 4ins. $1,400 £700

Edwardian mahogany grandfather clock with Westminster and Whittington chimes. 7ft 3ins. high. $1,430 £715

18th century mahogany cased grandfather clock by E. East $1,4 £720

German longcase clock (regulator) circa 1880, by Strasser and Rhode, in nutwood case with glazed front, 159cm. high. $1,440 £720

A George I black lacquer longcase clock, engraved S. Whicheote, London, 7ft. 3in. $1,440 £720

19th century oak longcase clock with Whittington and Westminster chimes. $1,440 £720

18th century design chiming longcase clock with satinwood inlay, 96in. high. $1,440 £720

Early 18th century black lacquered, 8 day longcase clock, with brass dial, by C. Stoddart. $1,440 £720

Heavily carved oak longcase clock with an 8 day musical chiming movement. $1,440 £720

Chiming longcase clock of late 18th century design, 96ins. $1,440 £720

An 18th century longcase clock, by J. Hewlett, Bristol, with an 8 day striking movement, in an inlaid and banded walnut case. $1,500 £750

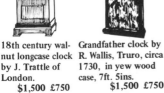

18th century walnut longcase clock by J. Trattle of London. $1,500 £750

Grandfather clock by R. Wallis, Truro, circa 1730, in yew wood case, 7ft. 5ins. $1,500 £750

19th century carved oak longcase clock with musical chiming movement. $1,500 £750

Mahogany longcase clock by T. Hackney of London, circa 1760. $1,500 £750

57

GRANDFATHER CLOCKS

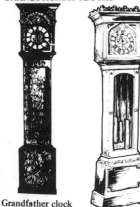

Grandfather clock by R. Wallis of Truro, 7ft 5 ins circa 1730. $1,510 £755

Victorian Gothic mahogany longcase clock with a silvered dial and Westminster chime. $1,520 £760

18th century green lacquered clock by John Jones of London. $1,560 £780

Edwardian inlaid mahogany longcase clock. $1,560 £78⬤

Good London mahogany 8 day longcase clock, circa 1770. $1,560 £780

Mahogany clock silvered dial by A. Thwaites of London. $1,570 £785

Mahogany longcase clock with an arch brass dial by Le Plastrier, London, circa 1790. $1,620 £810

Late 18th century Dutch walnut longcase clock. $1,680 £840

Walnut longcase clock by W. Owen, Llanrwst, 8 day movement, circa 1780. $1,680 £840

French longcase clock, circa 1830, in mahogany case, 188 cm high. $1,680 £840

18th century Dutch clock with English movement. $1,680 £840

An ebonised longcase clock, 8 day movement by John Wise of London, circa 1695 $1,680 £840

George II walnut longcase clock by T. Hunter of London. $1,700 £850

Mahogany longcase clock by E. Betts of Ipswich. $1,740 £870

Longcase regulator by Pennlington & Batty, with Graham dead beat escapement. $1,790 £895

A Georgian mahogany clock, inscribed Smorthwait Colchester. $1,800 £900

GRANDFATHER CLOCKS

18th century Chippendale style mahogany long-case clock with brass face and 8 day movement.
$1,800 £900

Highly decorative late 18th century French grand-father clock.
$1,800 £900

A fine 18th cen-tury marquetry longcase clock by Webster, Salop. $1,800
£900

A good quality mahogany longcase clock with a five pillar movement, b J. Smith, circa 178
$1,800

Mahogany longcase clock by Bowen, London, with strike/silent regu-lation, circa 1780.
$1,840 £920

Mahogany longcase clock converted to regulator by Brock-bank, Atkins & Moore in 1891. $1,860 £930

A black lacquer long-case clock, with repeating work by Winble of Ashford.
$1,860 £930

Cross-banded 18th century longcase clock, dial engraved Windmaills, London.
$1,870 £93

George III mahogany longcase clock with brass dial inscribed 'Thomas Brown'. $1,870 £935

Lacquer longcase clock by H. Hurt London, 12ins dial, 7ft 1in. $1,910 £955

Victorian free standing pedestal clock, 59½in. high $1,920 £960

Fine eight day clock by R. Cramp of Canterbury, circa 1770. $1,980 £990

Green lacquer longcase clock by Wm. Martin of Bristol, circa 1720. $1,980 £990

George III mahogany longcase clock, signed T. Mudge and W. Dutton. $2,040 £1,020

A mahogany longcase clock with 8 day movement by J. Ewer of London, circa 1760. $2,080 £1,040

Eight-day red lacquered clock by Brace of Chepstow. $2,090 £1,045

61

GRANDFATHER CLOCKS

Longcase clock by Delander, with arched dial and eight day movement. $2,100 £1,050

An 18th century longcase clock with brass dial and red gilt lacquered case, by T. Gorsuch, Salop. $2,110 £1,055

Three train longcase clock with moon phases, quarter chiming on either four or eight bells. $2,150 £1,075

Green lacquer longcase clock by Hall of London, the five pillar movement with strike/silent regulation. $2,160 £1,08

18th century walnut longcase clock by F. Conall of Lutterworth. $2,160 £1,080

18th century mahogany longcase clock by Wm. Hayley, Clerkenwell. $2,160 £1,080

A mahogany longcase regulator, the pendulum linked to the crutch by a roller. $2,160 £1,080

Blue lacquered longcase clock by A. Dunlop, London. 6ft 6ins. $2,160 £1

Black ebonised clock by T. Newman, Dublin, 11ins dial, circa 1700. $2,160 £1,080

An 18th century long-case clock in mahogany case, with striking lunar movement, inscribed Hartley, Norwich $2,160 £1,080

Longcase regulator with conventional silvered regulator dial, pulley offset and mercurial pendulum. $2,220 £1,110

Longcase regulator with silvered dial, mercurial pendulum and pulley offset. $2,220 £1,110

th century mahony cased regulator ock, inscribed 'F. Depree, Exeter. $2,220 £1,110

Green lacquer eight day clock by T. Bennet, London. $2,360 £1,180

18th century mahogany inlaid longcase clock, by J. Downie, Edin. $2,400 £1,200

A walnut cased symphonion disc clock/polyphone 6ft 6ins high. $2,400 £1,200

Fine longcase clock in a walnut case signed Windmills of London. $2,400 £1,200

Late 17th century marquetry longcase clock by William Weir of London. $2,520 £1,260

Early 18th century longcase month clock by George Etherington, with a matt brass dial, in an ebonised case. $2,520 £1,260

Fine longcase clock by Andrew Dunlop, in a lacquer case, circa 1720. $2,580 £1,2

Early 19th century mahogany longcase regulator, signed on dial, S. Marks, Cowbridge. $2,600 £1,300

Walnut and marquetry longcase clock by Thomas Bugden of Croydon, with a brass and silvered dial. $2,640 £1,320

Late 18th century mahogany longcase clock with eight day movement and brass dial, by J. Thwaite, Clerkenwell. $2,640 £1,320

Walnut longcase clock by Canno of London, with five-pillar move ment and strike silent regulator circa 1740. $2,640 £1,32

Early 18th century walnut and floral marquetry longcase clock by Sam. Wichell. $2,760 £1,380

Fine George III mahogany and satinwood longcase clock by R. Turner, Lewis. $2,760 £1,380

19th century longcase regulator, by Frodsham, with Graham dead-beat escapement, $2,800 £1,400

Fine walnut longcase clock by Jno. Speakman of London, circa 1710-1715. $2,880 £1,440

walnut longcase clock by Edward Speakman, London, 6ins. high. $2,880 £1,440

Early 18th century walnut and marquetry longcase clock by Robert Caldwell, London. $2,880 £1,440

Early 18th century Dutch longcase clock by Nicholas Dornheck of Amsterdam. $2,880 £1,440

18th century longcase clock by Samuel Stevens of London, in a fine marquetry case. $3,000 £1,500

An 18th century burr walnut longcase clock by J. Chater, London. $3,000 £1,500

A pollard oak and oyster walnut longcase clock by T. Ogden of Halifax, circa 1750. $3,000 £1,500

A longcase clock by J. Buffett of Colchester, with eight day movement. $3,000 £1,500

An 18th century longcase clock, with eight day striking movement by W. Mayhew, Woodbridge. $3,000 £1,5

Walnut longcase clock by A.M.Cressener, London. $3,000 £1,500

Edwardian mahogany grandfather clock. $3,000 £1,500

Maplewood longcase clock by T. Walker of Preston. $3,000 £1,500

18th century longcase clock by T. Wiswall, London 1780. $3,000 £1

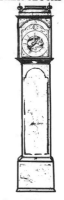

Mahogany long-case clock by Hilton-Wray of London, circa 1770. $3,040 £1,520

Walnut longcase clock, the five pillar movement with strike/silent regulation by Wentworth, London, circa 1750. $3,060 £1,530

17th century walnut longcase clock by R. Fenn of Westminster, 1690, $3,120 £1,560

Late 18th century red lacquered clock by C. Mauson of London. $3,120 £1,560

Edwardian chiming grandfather clock in a mahogany case ?ft. tall. $3,240 £1,620

A Continental longcase clock, decorated in the style of Teniers. $3,240 £1,620

A walnut longcase clock by H. Hindley of York. $3,240 £1,620

A mahogany longcase regulator of month duration, circa 1820. $3,300 £1,650

GRANDFATHER CLOCKS

Marquetry longcase clock by Samuel Hollyer, London, circa 1710. $3,300 £1,650

Longcase clock by Ellicott of London, circa 1750, in burr walnut case, 7ft. 5ins. high. $3,300 £1,650

A miniature longcase clock by O. Gardner of London with a weight driven movement, circa 1760, 4ft. 6in. high. $3,300 £1,650

An early 18th century walnut longcase clock by J. Weller. $3,300 £1,6

Late 17th century elm longcase clock by J. Martin of London, with an eight day movement. $3,300 £1,650

17th century longcase clock, the latched plates by Francis Coulton of London $3,300 £1,650

Mahogany longcase clock by Houlgrave, London, circa 1780, chiming the quarters on four bells. $3,410 £1,705

Early 18th century longcase clock in marquetry, inscribe 'Thos. Talbot, Nam twich', 210cm. hig $3,520 £1,76

17th century long-
case clock in a
walnut marquetry
case $3,520 £1,760

Late 18th century
floral marquetry
longcase clock, by
Christopher Gould.
$3,630 £1,815

George II longcase
clock in a fine
floral marquetry
case. $3,630 £1,815

Walnut and mar-
quetry eight day
longcase clock by
Peter Abbott of
London, circa
1695. $3,850 £1,925

Walnut longcase
clock by Hindley
of York, circa
1745, with dead-
beat escapement.
$3,850 £1,925

Walnut and
panelled scroll
marquetry long-
case clock by
Chris. Gould of
London, circa
1690.
$3,850 £1,925

Eight day longcase
clock, in walnut by
Claudius Duchesne,
London, 7ft. high.
Circa 1715.
$4,020 £2,010

William and Mary
walnut marquetry
longcase clock.
$4,070 £2,035

GRANDFATHER CLOCKS

George I
longcase clock
in an inlaid
floral mar-
quetry case.
$4,400
£2,200

George III regulator
inscribed 'Cragg,
Southampton'.
$4,400 £2,200

Mid 19th century
French marquetry
longcase clock in
a shaped case.
$4,400 £2,200

George III mahogan
longcase clock by
Vulliamy, London,
7ft. 1in. high.
$4,400 £2,2

Late 17th century
Dutch marquetry
longcase clock.
$4,400 £2,200

Walnut and marquetry
8 day longcase clock
by Jurigthoff of Bath.
$4,400 £2,200

Dutch walnut
longcase clock
by H. Ratsma,
Jnr.
$4,950 £2,475

Walnut and marquetr
clock by J. Windmills
Londini Fecit, circa
1695. $4,950 $2,47

Walnut and marquetry longcase clock by W. Wright of London, circa 1695. $5,500 £2,750

Dutch walnut marquetry inlaid longcase clock with bombe shaped base and domed hood by Van Meurs, Amsterdam. $5,720 £2,860

17th century brass lantern clock with a tic tac escapement in a period oak case. $5,720 £2,860

Early Dutch marquetry clock by F. Hauk, Rotterdam. $5,940 £2,970

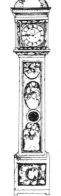

17th century month longcase marquetry clock by M. Ellwood of London, circa 1690. $6,050 £3,025

Louis XVI design pedestal clock with ormolu mounts. $6,050 £3,025

A marquetry longcase clock circa 1685. $6,160 £3,080

Mahogany striking grandather clock by R. Mathison, circa 1760. $6,160 £3,080

GRANDFATHER CLOCKS

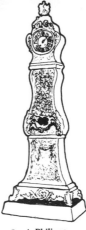

Walnut and marquetry longcase clock by H. Harper of London, circa 1695. $6,160 £3,080

Late 17th century marquetry longcase clock by T. Pare. $6,160 £3,080

Louis Philippe boulle clock, ormolu mounted. $6,380 £3,190

Slender walnut marquetry longcase clock, with 8 day movement. $6, £3,

A marquetry longcase clock by P. Penyston, circa 1690. $7,040 £3,520

A musical longcase clock, by H. Lough, Penrith, dated 1775. $7,040 £3,520

Longcase clock with 8 day movement by J. Wise, London, 11in. dial, circa 1695 $8,250 £4,125

Early 18th century marquetry longcase clock, b R. Williamson o London. $9,020 £4,5

Early 18th century musical and equation clock by W. Gibbs, 97ins. $9,900 £4,950

T. Mudge equation time-piece in a mahogany case. $18,260 £9,130

Longcase clock by R. Seignior of London, 7ft.1ins circa 1675. $20,900 £10,450

George II organ clock by Charles Clay of London, 2.5 metres high. $22,000 £11,000

Monthgoing long-case clock by G. Graham, London, circa 1715. $28,600 £14,300

A burr chestnut long-case clock by Tompion & Banger, circa 1704. $36,300 £18,150

A fine longcase clock by J. Knibb $39,600 £19,800

A small walnut long-case clock with 8 day movement, prior to 1680 by E. East, 5ft. 10in. $44,000 £22,000

LANTERN CLOCKS

A 19th century brass lantern clock with a carriage clock movement, 10ins. high. $110 £55

Victorian reproduction brass lantern clock with a French movement. $130 £65

Late 18th century brass lantern clock with enamel figures. $350 £175

17th century brass lantern clock with pendulum weights, and cord, by Henry Child, London, 16in. high. $430 £215

Brass lantern clock, dial engraved R. Rayment, 16 ins. $530 £265

18th century single-handed brass lantern clock by W. Cook of London. $740 £370

Fine 18th century brass lantern clock by W. Hatton of London. $780 £390

A fine lantern clock with an eight inch broken arch dial, inscribed Daniel Ray, Maningtree, 13in. high. $820 £410

An 18th century brass lantern clock, 12½ins high. $820 £410

74

Transitional lantern clock by Thomas Parker. $840 £420

A late 17th century lantern clock, the engraved dial signed Richd. Rayment, Bury, the movement restored. 1ft. 3½ins. high. $900 £450

Lantern clock by Richard Smith of Harlistone with an anchor escapement. $960 £480

17th century lantern clock by Peter Closson, with an 18th century anchor escapement conversion. $1,020 £510

A 17th century brass lantern clock by William Goodwin of Stowmarket. $1,200 £600

Lantern clock by T. Birch, London, with anchor escapement. $1,260 £630

A superb brass lantern clock, circa 1675. $1,820 £910

A wing lantern clock with a 6½in. dial signed Thomas West, London, 1ft. 3½in. high. $1,820 £910

Verge lantern clock by J. Ward, London, with back-plate but no doors. $1,860 £930

LANTERN CLOCKS

Brass lantern clock with original wing movement, 1670.
$1,920 £960

18th century brass lantern clock by John Crucefix, London. $2,000 £1,000

Wing lantern clock by Thomas Wheeler, circa 1680.$2,040 £1,0

A miniature lantern time-piece alarm by John Knibb, Oxon, with original verge escapement, 8ins. high, circa 1675. $2,400 £1,200

Winged lantern clock, by John Wise, London, with engraved wings and bellstrap. $3,300 £1,650

Lantern clock by William Selwood, with the original balance escapement, circa 1620. $4,400 £2,200

A rare striking lantern clock with original verge escapement by Daniel Quare, No. 72, circa 1690
$5,060 £2,530

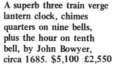

A superb three train verge lantern clock, chimes quarters on nine bells, plus the hour on tenth bell, by John Bowyer, circa 1685. $5,100 £2,550

A fine three train ting tang quarter striking chamber lantern clock by Johann Knibb, Oxon, 1690.
$15,400 £7,700

Plaster model of Windsor Castle painted in polychrome, inset with a clock, 22cm. wide. $24 £12

Late 19th century mahogany cased mantel clock. $30 £15

Victorian black marble mantel clock. $40 £20

A late 19th century brass 300 day clock under glass shade. $40 £20

A Jacobean style carved oak mantel chiming clock, with bronze mounts, 20ins. high. $40 £20

A Victorian marble drum head mantel clock, with an eight day movement, on an ebonised stand. $40 £20

Black and coloured marble mantel clock with French movement, 12½ins. high. $40 £20

An Edwardian mahogany mantel clock, by Elkington. $40 £20

Edwardian mantel clock in walnut case. $44 £22

MANTEL CLOCKS

A late Victorian oak cased mantel clock, with silverised dial and chiming movement, 15in. high. $50 £25

A 20th century mahogany chiming mantel clock with a silvered dial. $50 £25

Mantel timepiece in oak inlaid case. $50 £25

A late 19th century mahogany mantel timepiece, by Rattray, Dundee. $50 £25

Heavy black marble and brass mounted clock by 'Ansonia Clock Co.' U.S.A. $60 £30

A black coloured marble clock with bronze mounts, 20ins. high. $60 £30

19th century walnut cased mantel clock with an American movement. $60 £30

A Victorian mantel clock in black marble case, 14ins. high. $60 £30

19th century Victorian oak cased balloon shape clock. $60 £30

78

A fine Victorian mantel clock in mahogany inlaid case, 8¾ ins. high. $60 £30

Black marble mantel clock, 15ins. high. $60 £30

A 19th century carved and painted wood cuckoo clock. $64 £32

19th century oak cased striking clock decorated with carved dolphins. $64 £32

A mahogany mantel clock, with French eight day movement, and ebony inlay, 12in. high. $70 £35

Victorian black marble mantel clock. $70 £35

Edwardian oak cased striking clock by J.W. Bensen, Old Bond Street, London. $70 £35

Edwardian inlaid mahogany bracket clock. $70 £35

Victorian oak cased cuckoo clock, 18ins. high. $70 £35

79

MANTEL CLOCKS

19th century spelter mantel clock on a white alabaster base. $80 £40

Victorian inlaid mahogany mantel clock with serpentine shaped pediment, 11½ins. wide. $80 £40

A small 19th century plated timepiece on a wooden stand. $80 £40

A walnut cased mantel clock with chiming movement and silvered dial. $80 £40

Alabaster mantel clock with gilt metal dial and fluted pillars, 11ins. high. $84 £42

Victorian barometer and timepiece in a carved oak rope and anchor pattern case. $84 £42

A Victorian marble mantel clock in drum head, on shaped base with pillars, 18¾ ins. high. $90 £45

American mantel clock in carved wood case. $90 £45

Edwardian inlaid mahogany mantel clock with an eight day French movement. $92 £46

A timepiece in mahogany inlaid upright shaped case, 12ins. high. $92 £46

Late 19th century German mantel clock in an oak case. $92 £46

19th century soft metal French mantel clock, with white enamel dial, signed Hry. Marc, Paris. $100 £50

A mahogany inlaid lancet shaped mantel striking clock, on brass feet, 9½ins. high. $100 £50

Late 19th century French marble and spelter striking mantel clock. $100 £50

Mahogany inlaid lancet type mantel clock with French movement, 13ins. high. $110 £55

A mantel clock in black marble case with Ionic brass pillars and surmounted by a brass bust of Mercury, 8ins. wide. $110 £55

A French gilt metal mantel clock with acorn festoons, trumpets and armour in relief, and surmounted by a figure, 18ins. high. $120 £60

Walnut mantel clock with silverised and brass dial, 16ins. high. $120 £60

81

MANTEL CLOCKS

Edwardian mahogany carved mantel clock by Walker and Hall, 12ins. high. $120 £60

19th century French mantel timepiece 8ins. high. $120 £60

A fine 19th century American clock in a rosewood veneered case. $120 £60

Victorian eight day mantel clock in an oak case with brass finials. $120 £60

A mantel clock of Empire design in brass drum case, with flowers in relief, 9ins. high. $120 £60

19th century mantel clock in carved mahogany case with domed cornice, 17ins. high. $124 £62

An ebony, walnut and tortoiseshell cased mantel clock with brass and enamel dial, 11½ins. high. $124 £62

Regency eight day mantel clock with a mahogany and brass inlaid case. $130 £65

Victorian, Chinese style brass mantel clock, 18ins. high, with enamelled dial. $130 £65

Victorian lancet clock in a mahogany case with boxwood string inlay. **$150 £75**

A mantel clock with square brass and silvered dial, in oak case with carved domed hood, 25ins. high. **$150 £75**

Mahogany mantel clock with domed cover and brass handle, 14ins. **$160 £80**

19th century brass mantel clock surmounted by a cherub. **$160 £80**

An oval brass mantel clock, the French movement with white enamel dial contained in a moulded brass frame, 10ins. high. **$170 £85**

A 19th century mantel clock in walnut case with brass mounts, and silverised dial, 13ins. high. **$170 £85**

A gilt metal and china striking mantel clock, the painted dial with plaques, figures and flowers, 12½ins. high. **$170 £85**

Regency period mahogany cased clock with brass string inlay, with an eight day movement. **$190 £95**

19th century French ormolu clock of Louis XV style, 8½ins. high. **$200 £100**

83

MANTEL CLOCKS

A miniature carved oak longcase clock with chased brass and silvered dial, 1ft. 8ins. high. **$220 £110**

Unusual 19th century German barometer clock in an oak case. **$220 £110**

A brass and plate glass mantel clock, with white enamelled dial, by John Bennet, London, 15ins. high. **$240 £120**

19th century rouge marble mantel clock, mounted with two angelic metal figures, by Henri Marc of Paris. **$240 £120**

Gilt metal mantel clock in drum case on alabaster base and giltwood stand. **$240 £120**

19th century ormolu mantel clock with white porcelain face. **$240 £120**

Victorian alabaster mantel clock with an eight day French striking movement and large brass pendulum. **$240 £120**

An unusual 19th century French brass mantel clock. **$260 £130**

An interesting French night clock in the form of a vase. **$260 £130**

84

A fine brass Architectural clock in the style of one of the great London churches, 16ins. high. $260 £130

A 19th century French gilt metal and alabaster mantel clock, the movement flanked by the figure of an artist, 1ft. 8ins. high. $260 £130

Late 19th century Dresden mantel clock, with cherub side figures and surmount, 12ins. high. $260 £130

A French style gilt metal mantel clock surmounted by a Roman figure and a horse, 18ins. high. $280 £140

Large Victorian brass mantel clock with an eight day movement. $300 £150

A mantel clock in brass case with Ionic pillars and domed top, 16ins. high. $300 £150

Louis XV style mantel clock with white enamel dial, the plated case surmounted by a figure of a child, 16½ins. high. $340 £170

19th century French mantel clock in a mahogany case with ormolu decoration, 18ins. high. $340 £170

A fine rectangular clock with decorated porcelain panels and eight day movement. $340 £170

MANTEL CLOCKS

A French boulle and rosewood mantel clock, with chased brass mounts and feet, by H. Marr, Paris, 17ins. high. $360 £180

Brass inlaid Regency rosewood mantel clock, with silvered dial by Hill of Bristol. $360 £180

Regency rosewood 36 hour clock by Johnson of Reigate with ebony finial and feet, (signed and dated 1814). $370 £185

19th century French ormolu mantel clock with silk suspension. $370 £185

19th century French porcelain mantel clock complete with giltwood stand. $380 £190

A French mantel clock in tortoiseshell Louis XV shaped case with chased brass mounts, inscribed James Crichto & Co., 19ins. high. $41 £2

An unusual 19th century mahogany cased clock. $420 £210

Early 19th century French ormolu clock with an eight day movement, 14ins. high. $440 £220

An unusual 'Black Forest' fusee movement cuckoo clock. $44 £22

86

Early 19th century French architectural clock, under a glass dome. $440 £220

A French chased and repousse brass mantel clock, with drop handles and china dial, by Duven, Marsailles, 13½ ins. high. $440 £220

Louis XVI ormolu and marble mantel clock. $440 £220

Late 18th century bisquit de Sevres mantel clock, movement signed Felix Sandox, London, 11ins. high. $460 £230

A French mantel clock in tortoiseshell upright case with brass mounts, 13½ins. high. $460 £230

French mantel clock, the silvered dial engraved with makers name, Fearn a Paris, circa 1840, 12ins. high. $470 £235

Late 19th century French ormolu striking clock by Japy Freres, 15ins. high. $470 £235

19th century French striking mantel clock in ormolu with white enamel face. $480 £240

Regency period two train clock in an inlaid mahogany case. $480 £240

87

MANTEL CLOCKS

Mid 19th century mantel clock in the French rococo style, 12ins. high. $500 £250

A19th century marble clock, 32½ ins high. $550 £275

Late 18th century French brass mantel clock. $560 £280

84
5 80

Late Meissen clock case of architectural form, 13ins. high. $580 £290

An astronomical calendar clock in rouge marble, by Lister & Son, Newcastle. $600 £300

An early 19th century French lacquered mantel clock with ormolu mounts 13½ins. high. $600 £3

19th century French ormolu and white marble mantel clock, by Leroy, Paris, 22in. high. $650 £325

A Preiss clock in the Art Deco style. $660 £330

19th century French striking mantel clock with pink ground Sevres panels. $660 £330

19th century red boulle
and ebonised French
striking clock. $660
£330

Mid 19th century white
marble and ormolu clock
decorated with floral
swags, urns and beading,
13ins. high. $670 £335

Early Victorian
novelty timepiece
of painted pressed
tin. $700 £350

Mid 19th century white
marble and ormolu
mounted striking pillar
clock, 17ins. high. $710 £355

19th century French ormolu
and marble mantel clock.
$710 £355

English satinwood time-
piece by W. Hart and
Son, Cornhill, circa 1840,
9ins. high. $720 £360

19th century French
mantel clock with
ormolu decoration.
$720 £360

Large 19th century Dresden
striking clock encrusted with
flowers, 2ft 1ins. tall. $720
£360

An interesting 19th
century French
maritime clock.
$720 £360

MANTEL CLOCKS

Ormolu striking clock by Aubert and Klaftenberger of Geneva, inset with porcelain panels. $740 £370

A 19th century Austrian 'pendule d'officier', in an ormolu-mounted engine turned case, 5ins. high. $740 £370

19th century French ormolu clock with painted china dial, plaquettes and pillars, 17ins. high. $740 £370

Late 19th century clock with heavy ormolu mounts visible pendulum, and brass dial with raised chapter ring. $740 £370

A white alabaster mantel clock with vase surmount on an oblong base, with chased ormolu mounts. 2ft high, 1ft 6ins wide. $770 £385

Early 19th century eight day mantel clock with cloisonne decoration. $770 £38

19th century French champleve enamel clock. $770 £385

Early 19th century French alarm mechanism, in bronze case, standing on lion's paw feet, 5.8cm. $780 £390

French gilt mantel clock with decorative porcelai panels. $780 £39

An unusual Mariner's clock in brass and plate with a barograph and compass engraved Thomas Russell and Son, Paris. $780 £390

French ormolu striking clock with cupid mount and musical motif, 12ins. high, 12ins. wide, 5ins. deep. $780 £390

19th century French boulle clock, tortoise-shell case with brass inlay and ormolu mounts, 16in. $780 £390

Mid 19th century French mantel clock surmounted by a fine silver gilt bronze. $790 £395

19th century cloisonne and glass sided mantel clock with a mercurial pendulum. $790 £395

Boulle mantel clock, with hour and half-hour strike, by Vincenti, Paris, circa 1860, 12in. high. $800 £400

Cased clock, Strasbourg, signed by Aubinea, Strasbourg, in four cornered round metal case, depicting Strasbourg Cathedral $820 £410

A fine quality balloon shaped clock, in maho-gany case with brass string inlay, circa 1800. $820 £410

Victorian ebonised clock by Appleby, Dorchester, 24ins. high. $820 £410

MANTEL CLOCKS

An unusual 19th century Chinese fire clock, 6.25cm. long. $820 £410

A fine 19th century French ormolu mounted clock, 23½ in. high. $820 £410

19th century blue Sevres porcelain and ormolu clock by Leroy of Paris with original gilding. $830 £41

Hand painted blue porcelain and ormolu clock by Aubert and Klaftenburger of Geneva, circa 1850. $840 £420

Frederick Bull electric mantel clock in an arched rosewood case, 23cm. high, circa 1880 $840 £420

Mid 19th century whit onyx and ormolu mounted French striki clock. $850 £4

Mid 19th century French mantel clock with ormolu mounts. $860 £430

French bronze and ormolu clock, circa 1815. $860 £430

Very fine ormolu mantel clock with two train mov ment surmounted by a Cavalier figure, circa 183 $860 £43

19th century French
8 day clock mounted
on a bronze elephant
with a scrollwork
stand. $860 £430

A carved oak case mantel
clock with circular silverised dial and musical chiming
movement on eight bells, by
Payne & Co., New Bond St.,
London, 28½ in. $860 £430

Chariot timepiece
by James McCabe.
    $860 £430

Early 19th century French
mantel clock by Garrigues
of Paris. $880 £440

French ormolu and porce-
lain clock by Leroy of
Paris with putti, depicting a
hunting and fishing scene,
with original gilding. $900 £450

A walnut clock by
C. Frodsham of
London, circa 1830.
    $900 £450

19th century boulle and
ormolu mounted French
striking clock, 10ins. high.
    $940 £470

19th century French
lighthouse clock, 9½
ins. high. $940 £470

19th century French ormolu
striking clock by Japy Freres,
14in. high. $950 £475

MANTEL CLOCKS

19th century French ormolu striking mantel clock, 20½ ins high. $950 £475

French striking mantel clock in blue cloisonne and polychrome enamel, 17ins high. $950 £475

Regency ormolu mantel clock with a fine English movement, circa 1825. $960 £480

Early 19th century mantel clock by L. De Fils. $960 £480

George III neo classic bronze and ormolu mantel timepiece by Thomas Hawley. $1,020 £510

An early 19th century French boulle clock. $1,020 £510

A mantel or pedestal clock in the Louis XV manner by Leroy a Paris. $1,020 £510

A 19th century musical clock by Warren of London, in a brass inlaid case. $1,020 £510

18th century ormolu mantel clock, the dial and movement by "C. Baltazar a Paris", 13in. $1,030 £51.

French clock, circa 1820, by Leonce Pearl A Se Malo the face in ornamental glass, with cylinder movement, 29cm high.
$1,080 £540

A fine French ormolu chiming mantelpiece clock, the movement stamped Perrin, Paris, 24ins. high. $1,080 £540

Good quality red boulle mantel clock, circa 1830.
$1,080 £540

Bronze and ormolu Regency Fountain lock, circa 1810.
$1,080 £540

French ormolu clock by Adolphe Japy made for the French Great Exhibition in 1855. $1,080 £540

French striking clock by Howell and Cie and Vincenti of Paris, circa 1850, 14in. high. $1,080 £540

French bronze and ormolu mantel clock inscribed 'Renoir Paris'
$1,100 £550

Satinwood Director's clock. Striking Westminster and eight bell chimes with repeat. Inscribed Sir John Bennett, London.
$1,180 £590

An early 19th century automaton clock, signed on back Pepin a Paris, in ormolu case with marine design, 22ins. high. $1,180 £590

Regency period water-fall clock, with movement signed Chappe a Paris. $1,190 £595

Early 19th century French ormolu mantel clock $1,200 £600

French porcelain and ormolu mounted clock by M. I. Roy Freres, 19 ins. $1,200 £6

19th century French boulle striking clock, 24in. $1,200 £600

An unusual Austrian clock, striking hours and ¼ hours, circa 1840, 18 ins. $1,200 £600

Blue Sevres porcelain and ormolu French clock, circa 1850, 20 ins high, 16 ins wide, 6 ins deep. $1,200 £600

An ebonised mantel chronometer by T. Coombe, Brighton, 19.5 cm. $1,200 £600

Blue Sevres porcelain and ormolu mounted clock, circa 1860, 13 ins high, 11 ins wide, 6 ins deep. $1,200 £600

A burr walnut and brass inlaid mantel clock, by G. Makin & Sons, Manchester 11½ ins high. $1,200 £60

A Louis XV Cartel clock in tortoiseshell and brass. $1,260 £630

Unusual 19th century 'steam hammer' clock $1,260 £630

French mid 19th century boulle clock, 17 ins. $1,280 £640

Ebonised balloon clock by Leroux of London with a two train fusee movement of 8 day duration, circa 1770. $1,320 £660

19th century replica of an 18th century clock for the Middle East market. $1,320 £660

Louis XV mantel clock, with enamel numerals, mounted in ormolu, signed Etne Baillon a Paris, 19½ ins. $1,420 £710

Bronze and gilt French Bull clock. $1,440 £720

Georgian spring clock with 8 day fusee movement, inscribed W. Howse, London, 18½ ins high. $1,440 £720

German timepiece, circa 1680, by J. Piaff, Augsburg, with short pendulum at the back, 43 cm. high. $1,490 £745

97

Rare German itinerant clockmaker figure, carrying a clock on his chest, 13¾ ins. Late 18th century.
$1,560 £780

A 19th century French mantel clock with Orrery Globe rotating daily and imitating the earth's yearly axis deviation. $1,560 £780

Ships chronometer in a brass drum case on a mahogany base, by J. Hutton, London, 12½ ins. $1,620 £81

An important ormolu and Sevres style porcelain panelled clock by Japy & Sons of Paris, 20 ins high. $1,700 £850

19th century rosewood cased mantel clock, the backplate inscribed "Arnold Chas. Fordsham"
$1,700 £850

Victorian ormolu man clock with calendar an lever movement, the d inscribed by T. Agnew Sons. $1,750 £

A Charles X ormolu mantel clock. 37 cm. high. $1,780 £890

Louis XVI ormolu and black marble mantel clock with striking movement, signed Schmit a Paris. $1,920 £960

19th century Frenc bracket clock, inlai with tortoiseshell i the boulle manner. $2,090 £1,04

98

French ormolu
"snake-ring"
clock. $2,350 £1,175

Louis XVI boulle
bracket clock by
J. La Doux of
Amiens. $2,400 £1,200

Early 19th century
French ormolu clock,
circa 1810. $2,400 £1,200

Ornate ormolu and
veneered Louis XV
style mantel clock.
$2,520 £1,260

19th century Dresden
mantel clock decor-
ated with figures.
$2,520 £1,260

18th century gilt
metal striking
table clock with
verge escapement.
$2,640
£1,320

small 18th century
clock by Bunon a
aris, 73 cm. high.
$2,760 £1,380

French Exhibition clock
set in marble and ormolu
circa 1851. $2,900 £1,450

Louis XV clock by
F. Goyer veneered
in tortoiseshell and
cut brass, 4ft 1ins
tall. $2,900 £1,450

99

MANTEL CLOCKS

An ebonised clock by Fromanteel and Clarke, 18½ cm. $2,960 £1,480

A good clock, in red lacquered case, Neuenburg, circa 1830, 81 cm.
$2,900 £1,450

Mid 18th century gilt metal hexagonal table clock, signed Rellames, London. $2,960 £1,48

An 18th century boulle clock and bracket, in perfect condition, 3ft 8in high, 1ft 5in wide. $2,970 £1,485

A Napoleon I ormolu mounted 'bleu de roi' Sevres porcelain lyre clock by Collas of Paris. $3,520 £1,760

Longcase clock movement by Joseph Knibb with a brass dial, silver chapter ring and cherub spandrels.
$3,520 £1,76

18th century porcelain mounted French mantel clock, circa 1760, with figure ornament.
$3,570 £1,785

Ormolu and white statutory marble mantel clock by Raingo Freres, Paris, circa 1800, 95.4cm high.
$3,630 £1,815

Mahogany, musical thr train clock by Higgs & Diego Evans of Londo 30 ins. tall
$3,740 £1,87

Louis XVI ormolu and porcelain mantel clock with striking movement by Charles Dutertre. $3,850 £1,925

French 14 day musical clock circa 1800, by R.A. Dourles, 64cm. high. $4,000 £2,000

Louis XV globe mantel clock $4,180 £2,090

Renaissance tableclock, circa 1630, made in Augsburg, surmounted by a figure of the Goddess Fortuna. $4,200 £2,100

18th century English clock attributed to M. Boulton 1728-29 of Derbyshire Blue John with gilt metal mounts, 47 cm. $4,400 £2,200

An ormolu mantel clock by R. Philp of London 41 cm high $4,400 £2,200

A Karl Faberge silver gilt and mousse enamel boudoir timepiece $4,400 £2,200

Louis XV Boulle clock and bracket by Noel Baltazar of Paris $4,400 £2,200

A mantel clock by P. Lianne a Geneva, with ormolu mounts, striking on three bells, circa 1710, 85cm. $4,460 £2,230

MANTEL CLOCKS

A small clock, Augsburg, circa 1550, in gilded bronze case with religious motifs, 12.7cm.

$4,460 £2,230

Dial of a Quare and Horseman musical clock, case in poor condition.

$4,620 £2,310

French wall clock, circ 1740, by De Cleues a Paris, 115 cm.

$5,05
£2,52

French wall clock, in blue case decorated with floral design, circa 1770, 115cm. high.

$5,350 £2,675

18th century Dutch table clock in a tortoiseshell and a silver case, 13cm.

$5,500 £2,750

A fine clock by Foull Paris with gilded bro case, circa 1748, 83c

$5,9
£2,9

Mantel clock, with ormolu mounts, Paris, circa 1750, 115cm high. $5,940 £2,970

Wall clock, Paris 1740, in elegant case with polychrome floral decoration inlaid with horn and mother-of-pearl, striking on two bells, 125cm. high. $5,940 £2,970

Late Louis XIV bou bracket clock by Fr Lebaique, 3ft. 1½ins high, 1ft 10ins. wide

$6,000 £3,00

102

Musical clock by Le Mair of Amsterdam, the musical movement by Jan Hendrik Huhn, ringing on three bells, circa 1710, 114cm high. $7,000 £3,500

Mantel clock by Le Coeur a Paris, in veneered case, with figures, circa 1780, 122cm high.
$7,200 £3,600

Four pillared clock surmounted by an Orrery by Raingo of Paris, circa 1820.
$10,000 £5,000

A 17th century chaise clock watch by J. Barberet, Paris, 10cm. diam. $11,000 £5,500

Gilt metal mantel clock with an 18th century movement by Graham, 36cm high. $14,500 £7,250

A mid 17th century Prussian rectangular gilt metal table clock by George Schultz.
$18,500 £9,250

Ebony night clock by Edward East, circa 1670, 34ins. high.
$22,000 £11,000

An ebony cased table clock, with silvered chapter ring set against a finely matted ground, made by Edward East, circa 1665.
$42,000 £21,000

An Imperial Russian easter egg clock, by Michael Perchin, 8ins. high.
$180,000 £90,000

SKELETON CLOCKS

19th century brass skeleton clock under a glass case. $80 £40

Early 19th century brass skeleton clock, with strike, and a glass dome. $310 £155

Brass skeleton clock with silverised and pierced dial, 13¾in. high. $340 £170

19th century skeleton clock on a marble base. $360 £180

19th century brass skeleton clock on a platform base, 21ins. high. $360 £180

French skeleton alarm clock with engraved frame of type made for the 1851 Exhibition $370 £18

Victorian brass skeleton clock with a half second dead beat escapement. $380 £190

Passing strike, brass framed skeleton clock, on an ebony base. $440 £220

19th century skeleton timepiece, now rebase complete with dome. $480 £24

Small skeleton clock, with lyre shaped frame and five spoked wheels. $520 £260

An ivy leaf skeleton timepiece, with finely fretted frame. $530 £265

Small mid-19th century English skeleton timepiece, with five spoked wheels and skeletonised barrel. $540 £270

19th century six-pillar single chain fusee skeleton timepiece with engraved dial, 11½ ins. $590 £295

19th century Gothic design skeleton clock complete with a glass dome, circa 1855. $600 £300

Small early 19th century scroll design, hour striking skeleton clock $660 £330

Regency brass 'Brighton Pavilion' two train skeleton clock. $720 £360

A two train skeleton clock by Moore of Worthing. $780 £390

A fine striking skeleton clock, with engraved frame. $780 £390

105

SKELETON CLOCKS

Fine quality 19th century small size two train skeleton clock of Cathedral design. $830 £415

Rare skeleton clock with twenty-four hour dial. $880 £440

19th century brass skeleton clock with subsidiary dials. $950 £475

Brass skeleton clock by R. Morrison of Inverness, 15ins. high. $960 £480

A fine skeleton timepiece, with five spoked wheels, skeletonised spring barrel and lever escapement. $1,020 £510

An exceptional (Brighton Pavilion) skeleton clock with a two train eight day movement, 20 ins. $1,100 £55

English double fusee skeleton clock of Lichfield Cathedral pattern. $1,200 £600

Mid-19th century striking and repeating English skeleton clock with six spoke wheels by Pearce and Sons. $2,000 £1,000

A magnificent Victor skeleton clock set on marble base. $3,200 £1,6

Smiths eight day wall clock in a brass case. $60 £30

Victorian circular wall clock by Jump, London. $60 £30

A Victorian wall clock in brass case, mounted on a decorated ware wall plaque. $70 £35

American wall clock by Jerome and Co., New Haven, Connecticut. $70 £35

A wall clock, with enamel dial, in a fine rosewood case, by J. & D. Meek, Edinburgh. $70 £35

Victorian rosewood octagonal wall clock. $80 £40

A stained wood cased wall clock with circular enamelled dial, by Llewellins, Bristol. $84 £42

19th century wall clock with a thirty hour movement. $84 £42

Victorian mahogany cased wall clock with an enamelled dial, by Gaydon & Sons, Kingston upon Thames. $84 £42

WALL CLOCKS

Late 19th century American regulator wall clock. $84 £42

George III mahogany wall clock with an 8 day movement and enamel dial.
$100 £50

A walnut inlaid wall clock with enamelled dial.
$100 £50

Regency mahogany and brass inlaid wall clock , 1ft. 11 ins. $110 £55

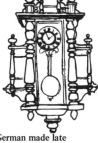

German made late Victorian clock. $120 £60

19th century mahogany framed regulator wall clock. $120 £60

Victorian walnut and floral marquetry wall clock with enamel dial.
$120 £60

An American walnut wall clock with glazed door. $130 £65

Wall clock with circular yew frame with black roman numerals. $130 £65

Regency period
rosewood, octa-
gonal wall clock
inlaid with brass.
$144 £72

Regency period Parliament
clock in a mounted rosewood
case. $160 £80

Late 18th century
mahogany wall
clock with a 16in.
dial. $160 £80

Victorian regulator
wall clock in a
mahogany case.
$170 £85

Drop dial clock by Eagleton,
Norwich, with a rosewood case
inlaid with mother-of-pearl.
$170 £85

A Victorian wal-
nut cased wall
clock with
fluted pillars,
enamel dial and
brass pendulum.
$170 £85

Late 19th century
papier mache wall
clock with mother-
of-pearl decoration.
$180 £90

Victorian eight day
regulator wall clock.
$200 £100

19th century mahogany
cased fusee movement
wall clock with a quar-
ter strike. $200 £100

18th century Continental wall clock in a walnut case.
$200 £100

A carved walnut and ebonised cased wall clock, with enamel circular dial, 4ft.4ins.
$220 £110

Viennese mahogany regulator timepiece, circa 1860. $240 £120

Early 19th century drop dial wall clock with full hour strike and two train movement.
$240 £120

Hooded alarm wall clock by Whitmore of Northampton with two independent trains, 22 ins.
$250 £125

Two train striking mahogany cased wall clock, by Pearson of Towcester, circa 1820. $250 £125

Mahogany wall clock with convex dial and glass. $280 £140

Rare Norfolk miniature wall clock in a flame mahogany case with 8 day movement. 35 ins overall. $350 £175

Early 19th century hooded wall alarm clock by T. Will Hay, Shrewsbury, 32 ins. $350 £175

Oak cased tavern clock by Abbot of London, circa 1790, with 8 day movement.
$410 £205

Attractive and well-figured walnut striking Vienna regulator. $440 £220

An unusual musical picture clock depicting the Houses of Parliament, circa 1870.
$440 £220

"Salt box" oak-cased wall clock, by W. Anness of Cheapside, London, with finely engraved dial and anchor escapement.
$470 £235

An Act of Parliament clock by W. Harris, Chipingham, in lacquered case, circa 1770, 60 ins. $480 £240

Mid 18th century brass faced wall clock with a 30 hour movement.
$480 £240

19th century boulle wall clock with fine ormolu enrichments.
$480 £240

19th century eight day red boulle wall clock with ormolu decoration. $480 £240

Continental wall clock with an enamel dial and pressed brass decoration. £500 £250

111

WALL CLOCKS

A fine 19th century Act of Parliament clock. $540 £270

A very fine mahogany wall regulator with six pillar movement. $780 £390

Late 18th century mahogany weight-driven wall clock with silverised dial. $800 £400

Japanese pillar clock timepiece, circa 1800. $840 £420

Late 18 century Act of Parliament clock, with black ground carrying gilt chinoiserie decoration. $860 £430

London silverised dial mahogany verge wall clock by Thornton, circa 1790. $880 £440

Small eight day tavern timepiece, circa 1790, in a lacquer case, 42in. long. $880 £440

Rare brass wall clock by P. Guy of Liverpool, circa 1700. $910 £455

Rare Japanese miniature pillar clock, 9½ ins, circa 1800. $920 £460

Small wall clock signed W. Simcox, London, with verge escapement and alarm, 4½ ins face, circa 1674. $1,020 £510

Louis XV ormolu cartel clock of scrolling foliate design, the case stamped Germain, 16ins. high.

$1,200 £600

A Liberty silver and enamel clock, Birmingham 1905, its borders decorated with stylised leaves, 8 ins. $1,200 £600

18th century Act of Parliament clock in black and gold lacquered case, inscribed T. Green, 5ft 4 ins. $1,220 £610

17th century Frisian wall clock. $1,250 £625

A fine Act of Parliament clock by Johnson of Grays Inn Passage, with two-week movement, circa 1780. $1,430 £715

Act of Parliament clock. $1,490 £745

Early 19th century, small French wall clock, by Leroy a Paris, of ormolu, with a gilded decorative face, 19.5cm diam. $1,510 £755

18th century Act of Parliament clock by J. Wilson of Stamford. $1,550 £775

113

WALL CLOCKS

A green lacquered Stage Coach House, Act of Parliament clock, by T. Wright, London, 1780. $1,620 £810

Act of Parliament clock by T. Wright, London, 1780, of 8 day duration. $1,680 £840

French ormolu cartel clock, circa 1840, 4ft 5½ ins high. $1,800 £900

Square wall clock by Charles Rennie Mackintosh, 15in. square. $3,000 £1,500

Walnut Viennese regulator by Lenzkirsch. $2,200 £1,100

French wall clock, circa 1790, with ormolu mounts, 79 cm high. $3,200 £1,600

Tavern clock with a 24 hour dial, the hour hand showing the time for 24 places around the world. $3,300 £1,650

A rare organ clock with an Austrian case and clockwork, circa 1760, and an English organ, circa 1735. $3,520 £1,760

Louis XV period wall clock in ormolu, the dial signed "Fieffe de l'observatoir". $35,200 £17,600

114

Late Victorian man's pocket watch in good working order. $28 £14

Victorian silver pocket watch in a delicately chased case. $54 £27

Unusual gun metal watch set on a bar brooch. $72 £36

Heart shaped silver watch decorated with alternate stripes of engraved silver and plain pink gold overlay. $180 £90

A P. Phillipe & Co. chronometer in an 18ct gold case. $260 £130

A gold keyless lever chronograph from the late 19th century.
$310 £155

A gilt metal cased pedometer and compass by Fraser, circa 1800. $340 £170

A gold pair cased quarter repeating ruby cylinder watch by E. Norton of London, circa 1790.
$360 £180

William IV pair cased silver pocket watch by G. Coxon of Oldbury, hallmarked for 1836.
$430 £215

George II pair cased watch, movement by W. Baker of London, circa 1779. $440 £220

Large 19th century French astronomical pocket watch with decorated face, date month and moon phase apertures, 7.7cm. $460 £230

19th century Swiss time-piece, cased in crystal and broad metal, 6.5cm. diam. $460 £230

Gold and black enamel lever dress watch by Longines. $500 £250

Gold pocket watch, Swiss, circa 1800, by Coulin of Geneva, in plain gold case, 5.3cm. diam. $520 £260

Gilt metal and enamel verge watch by J. Leroy of Paris. $580 £290

Silver pocketwatch by 'D.D. Neweren, London', circa 1760, enamel dial. $600 £300

A gold Massey lever watch by M.I. Tobias of Liverpool, circa 1830. $650 £325

18ct. gold hunter lever stopwatch with gold compensation balance by R. Roskell of Liver-pool, 1822. $660 £330

18ct. gold cased keyless lever chronograph by U. Nardin. $670 £335

English silver pocket watch circa 1880, in smooth case engraved on outer case with mythological scenes, 4.6cm. diam. $710 £355

An attractive gold hunting cased lady's keyless cylinder watch. $720 £360

19th century cylinder watch with engraved floral and architectural decoration. $770 £385

A gold cased quarter repeating duplex watch by Leplastrier of London, hallmarked 1823. $860 £430

18ct. gold pocket watch by T. Mudge with an embossed gold outer case. $860 £430

Gold and enamel half hunting cased keyless cylinder watch by P. Philippe of Geneva. $860 £430

Silver pair cased watch by Ninyan Burleigh. $860 £430

French gold watch, circa 1820, in smooth case with white and blue figures, 5.2cm. diam. $970 £485

WATCHES

Silver pocketwatch, Swiss, circa 1895, in engraved case, the face having Arabic numerals, 7.4cm. long.
$970 £485

A gold verge watch by Dubois et Fils with polychrome enamel dial plate, circa 1790.
$1,010 £505

George III gold watch by Barber of London.
$1,080
£540

Gold hunting watch, circa 1900, signed on face, Audemars Freres, Geneva, with chronograph indicator in the centre, 5.6cm. diam.
$1,090 £545

A silver triangular keyless lever watch by Schwab and Brandt of Switzerland. $1,090 £545

Gold timepiece, the case decorated with musical instruments and flowers, with gold hands, 4cm. diam.
$1,130 £565

Silver pocketwatch by A.S. & F. Mysterieuse, Brevete, 1888, in smooth silver case both sides finely engraved, with cylinder movement, 5.3cm. diam. $1,130 £565

French, two-coloured gold pocketwatch, circa 1780, the face having Arabic numerals and gold hands, 3.8cm. diam.
$1,130 £565

Gold cased keyless mystery watch signed Mysterieuse, Brevete, S.G.O.G. $1,250 £62

118

Gold and enamel verge watch by C. Leroy of Paris, circa 1780.
$1,250 £625

Swiss timepiece, circa 1790, in gilded case, in polychrome a young couple, 5.8 cm. diam.
$1,300 £650

English pocketwatch, circa 1740, the outer gold case, decorated with a mythological scene. $1,360 £680

A minute repeating lever watch by Dent in a gold case set with rose diamonds, 1866. $1,390 £695

A gold quarter repeating verge watch by Vacheron & Constantin of Geneva, circa 1820. $1,440 £720

Gilt metal verge clock watch by E. Price of London, circa 1720.
$1,440 £720

Pendant watch, Swiss, circa 1820, by Bernand & St. Croix, the case set with green leaves and rubies, 3.8cm. long. $1,460 £730

French pocket watch by Giradier, in pinchbeck case with painted dial and paste border. $1,490 £745

Silver pocket watch, circa 1820, with decoratively worked face, 5.4cm diam.
$1,550 £775

119

Swiss pocketwatch, circa 1700, signed by D. Jean Irchard, in smooth case, one of the makers best works, 5.3cm. diam.
$1,620 £810

Four coloured gold watch French, circa 1780, in engraved case, on the back an oval miniature of a young girl, 4.1 cm. diam.
$1,620 £810

A gold quarter repeating virgule watch circa 1840.
$1,630 £815

Mid 18th century quarter repeating verge watch by J. Gerrard of London in a gold pair case. **$1,680 £840**

18th century silver Oignon watch with a calendar dial.
$1,680 £840

Austrian silver and enamel table watch inscribed 'Luis Schudulin a Wien'. **$1,680 £8**

English gold pocketwatch circa 1770, the outer case decorated with a mythical scene in relief, 4.7cm diam. **$1,780 £890**

Early 19th century detached double roller lever watch hallmarked 1822. **$1,800 £900**

Pair cased silver pocketwatch by 'Cabrier, London', case by Cochin, circa 1750. **$1,880 £94**

Swiss gold watch set with paste and decorated with three coloured gold, circa 1775. $1,920 £960

Silver pocketwatch with date aperture, English, circa 1770, with silver face bearing small signature, 5.5cm diam.
$1,940 £970

18th century gold watch with quarter repeater, in initialled case, signed inside, 4.5cm. $1,940 £970

Silver pocketwatch with date aperture, Dutch, circa 1740, with silver figured face, also with sun and moon apertures 4.8cm. diam. $2,100 £1,050

Large gold wristwatch, Paris, circa 1820, in round case, finely engraved with flowers.
$2,100 £1,050

Early 19th century independent seconds, quarter repeating cylinder watch by Lepine of Paris. $2,160 £1,080

Gold hunting watch with a chronograph, with five second hands, Danish, circa 1860, 5.3cm. diam. $2,270 £1,135

Gold pocketwatch in two leafs, French circa 1800, in smooth walled case with date and week indicators. 5.2cm. diam. $2,270 £1,135

Astronomical silver pocket watch, English, circa 1750, in smooth case with gilded face, with three silver gilt rings, date and month indicator, 4.5cm. diam. $2,270 £1,135

121

English pocketwatch, circa 1680, in smooth silver case, with silver face, having a pendulum, 5.4cm diam.
$2,270 £1,135

Gold hunting watch, signed by Martin of Geneva, in ornamental case, with chain set with turquoises, 4.2cm diam.
$2,400 £1,200

Swiss made gold watch with pearls set round the edges of smooth case, 5.9cm high circa 1830.
$2,380 £1,190

A gold and enamel quarter repeating watch by Gudin of Paris, hallmarked 1777. $2,420 £1,210

Gold minute keyless lever chronograph by A. Piquet of Geneva. $2,420 £1,210

Silver pocket watch, with large minute hand in the centre on the bridge of the spindle, diam. 5.6cm.
$2,520 £1,260

A repousse gold pair cased verge watch by Swayne of London, hallmarked 1727.
$2,640 £1,320

Timepiece, circa 1680, German filigree bronze case formed with rosettes, 6cm. diam.
$2,970 £1,485

Gilt metal and enamel hour repeating cylinder watch by Wm. Carpenter, London, circa 1790.
$3,700 £1,850

English gold watch with quarter repeater, circa 1760, the case set with precious stones, with spindle movement, 4.7 cm. high. $3,860 £1.930

An exhibition example timepiece with figured face bearing signature of Breguet & Son, circa 1802, 5.4cm. $4,160 £2,080

A chaise watch by Gabrier, London, in a silver case, circa 1740. $4,180 £2,090

Gold, musical watch, circa 1820, neck and handle set with large pearls, enamelled with floral decoration, with cylinder movement, 6.2 cm. high. $4,750 £2,375

An early pocket chronometer by Wright of London 1784, no 2228. $8,140 £4,070

Gold pair cased verge watch by Baronneau of Paris, mid 17th century. $9,240 £4,620

Gold and enamel pair cased quarter repeating cylinder watch with chatelaine. $9,240 £4,620

Swiss gold enamelled and diamond set chime repeating clock watch, painted with a tiger attacking an Indian horseman. $11,090 £5,545

English silver pair cased verge clock watch, signed R. Seignor, London. 4½ ins diam. $21,250 £10,625

123

INDEX